THE YOUNG
Field Archaeologist's
GUIDE

by John X. W. P. Corcoran
F.S.A.

LONDON
G. Bell and Sons, Ltd
1966

Printed in Great Britain by
Richard Clay (The Chaucer Press), Ltd., Bungay, Suffolk

Contents

PLATES

opposite page

Contents

Preface

OUR past history may be read in books. It may also be read out of doors in ancient monuments. We are particularly fortunate in these islands in having many thousands of remains of ancient structures which are easily visited, but sometimes less easily understood. This book describes the principal field monuments of Britain and Ireland so that a young person seeing the remains of a stone structure or an earthwork may recognise it for what it is and understand its original purpose. In this way it is hoped that the reader of this book may acquire a heightened awareness of the man-made treasures of his countryside's past. The book also attempts something more. The Archaeology of these islands will not be written fully for many centuries to come if, indeed, it is ever fully written. Many new discoveries are made in the field each year, and it has long been one of the strengths of British and Irish Archaeology that amateur archaeologists have played a considerable part in this. Field archaeology, then, is something more than the passive appreciation of the remains of the past. It offers the opportunity of contributing to knowledge, and some of the means by which this may be achieved are discussed in this book. There are no age limits set on those who wish to participate. Those who begin when still young may find offered to them an absorbing interest for the rest of their lives, even if they do not wish to make a career of Archaeology.

Kilmaurs,
Ayrshire
May 1965

to T. G. E. P. who taught me so much

CHAPTER I

Archaeology and Field Work

IN 1879 a young Spanish girl, María De Sautuola, had accompanied her father, who was digging for prehistoric remains, into a cave. Losing interest in her father's work, María wandered a short distance away and suddenly she saw that the ceiling of the cave was covered with paintings of large animals. 'Father, father,' she shouted, 'look, painted bulls!!' María was the first person for thousands of years to see the now famous cave paintings of Altamira in northern Spain.

In September 1940 a young French boy, Ravidat, out in the woods with some friends, saw his dog, Robot, disappear into the ground. Following the dog, Ravidat slithered down a crack into a cave. Fortunately he had a torch with him, and called his friends to come down. Exploring the cave, they found that the walls and ceiling were decorated with painted animals. The cave paintings of Lascaux in south-western France had been discovered.

These young people may properly be called field archaeologists. They observed and they reported what they had seen. Admittedly, María merely had to shout to her father, who was only a few yards away, but he had been working in that cave for days without seeing the paintings. María used her eyes, and what we know as Palaeolithic cave art was discovered. Ravidat and his friends lived in an area of France, the Périgord, which by 1940 was already famous for similar cave

paintings, and they were immediately able to recognise
what they had discovered. María was mistaken,
understandably mistaken, in shouting, 'look, painted
bulls!!', as for many centuries nobody had seen prehistoric painted bison—for that is what she had seen.
In the years between 1879 and 1940 archaeologists had
been studying cave paintings, and Ravidat and his
friends were able to draw on this accumulated knowledge and so appreciate the significance of their discovery in a way that was impossible for María or her
father.

A simple definition of *Archaeology* is the study and
interpretation of the material remains of the past.
Every work in this definition is important and must be
taken literally. By the 'past' we do not mean only the
distant and remote past, but include in it all periods
since the beginning of Man to the present century. In
a sense the past begins yesterday. Material remains
include everything from small objects, such as coins,
flint tools and pieces of broken pottery, to large structures, such as Roman forts, disused railways and castles.
We study all these things so that we may understand
something of how people lived in the past. We should
not be mere collectors, either of objects or of facts. To
be of value these things must be interpreted, so that
gradually more and more information may be put
together from their study, and so enable us to visualise
what tools were used, what sort of houses were lived in,
what people wore and ate throughout the hundreds of
centuries of Man's existence on earth.

It may seem strange at first sight that the material
remains of recent centuries should be the concern of
archaeologists. It might be thought, as we have so
much written evidence, that the study of material
remains would add little to what is known of the past

derived from records written at the time. We may best appreciate this if we examine the many subdivisions of Archaeology. We speak, for example, of Classical Archaeology, Medieval Archaeology and Industrial Archaeology. *Classical Archaeology* is concerned with remains of the classical civilisations of the Greeks and Romans, *Medieval Archaeology* with the remains of the Middle Ages in Europe from the end of the Roman Empire to about the sixteenth century A.D. *Industrial Archaeology* is the most recently defined subdivision, and it is concerned with the disused remains of early factory sites, machinery and transport dating from the beginnings of the Industrial Revolution, that is from about the eighteenth century A.D. onwards.

In each of these periods of time archaeological studies supplement the work of historians who deal with written evidence from the period in question. Written records, however, go back no farther in time than about 5,000 years ago to a period around 3000 B.C. when writing was first invented in the Middle East. This does not mean that written records were in use throughout the world from that time onwards. In England, for example, the use of written records begins with the Roman period, a little under 2,000 years ago. In Australia written records begin in the eighteenth century A.D., and in some parts of the Far East only in the present century.

Even if we take the beginnings of written records back to 3000 B.C., there is still a very long period of time during which Man was without written history. This means that we can never hope to find any account of events written down in any part of the world before 3000 B.C. It does not mean that we can know nothing of everyday life during that period, for material remains survive from the earliest times of Man's existence. We are dependent, however, on material remains alone in any attempt to reconstruct the remote past, unlike the study of the historic past in which the study of written and archaeological evidence supplement each other.

The subdivision which is concerned with the material remains of the period before History is known as *Prehistoric Archaeology*. *Prehistory* may be defined as the period before the use of written records. It is often incorrectly identified with Archaeology as a whole, but as we know, Archaeology is concerned with the material remains of all periods, including the most recent. We have also seen that written records came into use at different times in different parts of the world. From this it follows that the prehistoric period ends at different times. In southern England, for example, the prehistoric period ends in A.D. 43 with the arrival of the Romans, in Australia in A.D. 1788, when Sydney was founded.

In those parts of the world where written records date from 2000 or 3000 B.C. the prehistoric period extended over a duration of time very much longer than the longest historic period. Present evidence suggests that Man as a tool-making creature appeared one million or more years ago. Set against this vast period of time, the historic period in any part of the world accounts for a very small fraction of Man's past. To help us to understand Prehistory it is customary to divide it into three periods, the Stone Age, the Bronze Age and the Iron Age, named after the most important material in use at the time for the manufacture of tools and weapons. The Stone Age came first, and it may be divided into the Old Stone Age and the New Stone Age. The *Old Stone Age*, or the *Palaeolithic* period, as it is usually called, embraces the time from Man's first appearance to the beginnings of farming. The *New Stone Age*, or *Neolithic* period, covers the time when Man was a farmer, but before he had learned how to cast metal. In certain parts of the world a third division, the *Middle Stone Age*, or *Mesolithic* period, is sometimes inserted between the two. The Bronze and Iron Ages explain themselves, although it should be remembered that tools continued to be made of stone, alongside copper, bronze and iron, for a long time after metal came into use.

We speak of the Stone Age, the Bronze Age and the Iron Age, but these did not occur simultaneously in all parts of the world. It would be more correct to speak of Stone, Bronze and Iron *stages*, as they really refer to certain levels of technological development and not to a fixed period of time, in the sense that we speak of the Victorian period. As the historic period began at different times in different parts of the world, so did the Neolithic and the Bronze and Iron Ages begin and end at different times. This was because certain important discoveries, such as the domestication of animals, the growing of crops and metalworking, were made in relatively few parts of the world and the new knowledge had to spread from these places. New knowledge spread sometimes rapidly, sometimes very slowly, so that some peoples even in more recent historic times knew nothing of farming or of metalworking.

In general, the greater part of Europe and Asia passed through the Stone, Bronze and Iron Ages, and this is true of the British Isles. In this book we are concentrating on field archaeology in Britain and Ireland, but we must remember that archaeological study embraces the world as a whole. The study of the past in the Americas includes the great Aztec, Inca and Maya

civilisations in Central America, as well as the materi-
ally less advanced early peoples of North and South
America. India, the Far East, Australasia and the
Pacific each has its Prehistoric Archaeology. The
basic techniques of Archaeology apply to all areas,
although detailed interpretation requires great specialised knowledge, which may be acquired only by long
study of the relevant archaeological material.

Our concern, then, is with the Field Archaeology of
the British Isles. By *Field Archaeology* we mean the
study of the material remains of the past which are to
be found out of doors. This includes examination of
archaeological sites and the recognition of small objects
which may be found lying on the ground or be uncovered either by natural action, as when a storm
causes sand to shift, or by Man's activities, such as
ploughing or bulldozing. To be consistent, archaeological excavation should properly be included, as it is
pre-eminently concerned with the study of material
remains in the open air, but it is normally regarded as
being distinct from field work or, as it might be termed,
field reconnaisance. Archaeological excavation involves a number of highly specialised techniques, which
may be learned only by training and experience under
careful tuition on an actual excavation. As such, we
shall not concern ourselves with it in this book.

Our definition of Archaeology emphasised that
material remains must be interpreted if they are to be
of any value. An archaeologist therefore cannot be
merely a field archaeologist. He cannot properly
recognise sites in the field if he does not have some basic
knowledge of their purpose and some appreciation of
their position in time. To acquire this knowledge he
must study books on Archaeology and examine museum
collections. In the following chapters we shall con-

sider certain types of monuments and smaller, portable objects.

At once we shall see that there are differences in approach to the remains of the prehistoric period and those of later times. We have fixed dates in history such as battles—Hastings in A.D. 1066, Clontarf in A.D. 1014 and Culloden in A.D. 1746. We know when kings and queens came to the throne. Knowledge of these dates, which have come down to us by written records, gives us our chronology. *Chronology* means giving dates to events, dates expressed in terms of a calendar, as in the case of the battles just mentioned. This is termed *absolute chronology*. Chronology also means the arrangement of events within a time sequence, such as saying that the Romans were in Britain before the Anglo-Saxons came, and that both peoples lived before the motorcar was invented. It does not tell us when the motorcar was invented or when the Romans and Anglo-Saxons lived, but it does tell us which came first, second and third within a chronological sequence. In the historic period we may reasonably expect to have the help of absolute chronology. We may know, for example, that a certain castle was built in the reign of a certain king. For much of the prehistoric period we often have to be content with relative chronology, to know that a certain group of people lived in the British Isles before the arrival of a second group. With recent development of scientific methods of dating, however, it is becoming increasingly possible to assign approximate dates, often to within a century, to certain developments. This is particularly true of the *later prehistoric period*, that is the Neolithic, Bronze and Iron Ages.

There is a second fundamental difference between the prehistoric and historic periods. Whereas in history we may speak of William the Conqueror or Robert the Bruce, Owen Glendwyr or Brian Boru, in Prehistory we are dealing with groups of peoples whose names we can never know because they did not write. That is why we speak of the 'Beaker folk', 'chambered cairn builders' and the like. These are the names of archaeological cultures. In this context a *culture* is defined as a number of objects, which may include both structures and portable objects, frequently occurring together in a number of distinct places within a certain geographical area. This is a clumsy definition, but if we take a particular example we may more easily see what it means. The Windmill Hill Culture is known in the south of England from its long earthen burial mounds, its flint mines and large enclosures marked by surrounding banks and ditches. Certain well-defined types of pottery, flint, bone and antler tools have been found at these sites, which are mainly concentrated on the upland chalk areas of Wiltshire and neighbouring counties. Their study allows us to see something of the way of life of these Neolithic farming people. In this example culture might also be given its broader meaning of the *whole* way of life of a people, but many archaeological cultures at present do not offer such a detailed picture. Because we do not know the name of these people we refer to the Windmill Hill Culture. In this example the name is taken from a site near Avebury in Wiltshire where this archaeological culture was first recognised. This is termed a *type site*. Sometimes cultures are named after one of the distinctive objects found on their sites, such as the Beaker folk, whose drinking vessels have frequently been found with their burials. Other cultures are known simply by titles, such as Iron Age A, B, C, Late Bronze Age I and II and so on.

From this we should not assume that the study of Prehistoric Archaeology merely involves the setting-out in a chronological sequence of a succession of sites and their associated small finds.   It is now becoming possible to reconstruct a great deal of the life of prehistoric man in the British Isles, particularly from the Neolithic onwards—his economy, his skills, something of his ritual life, trade and warfare.   Similarly, the archaeological contribution to the historic period has proved to have been of considerable value.   In the past we have tended to know more of the great affairs of state, of kings, of treaties and of battles, because it was these which seemed significant to the chroniclers of the day. The life of the ordinary people was thought less worthy of note.   Archaeology is helping to provide a more rounded picture of the more recent past, and not only for the Middle Ages.   In recent years, for example, field work and a limited amount of excavation, based on the results of field work, have begun to give us more detail of the way of life of the eighteenth and nineteenth centuries A.D. in the Highlands of Scotland.

An essential preliminary to much archaeological research is provided by field work.   Without information provided by field survey, it would be impossible to plan a satisfactory excavation.   If an archaeologist wishes to excavate a certain type of site he has to examine the possibilities of several sites of that type before he can decide on which site to excavate.   This may be achieved only on the basis of preliminary field surveys, either carried out entirely by himself or partly based on published accounts of other archaeologists. From this he is able to decide which site offers the greatest likelihood of providing the relevant answers to his questions, for all archaeological excavation should aim to solve specific archaeological problems.   Field work would reveal information such as which sites were least disturbed. It would also show the geographical relationship of particular sites to the group as a whole, so that if some sites lay near the coast and others inland, for example, he would gain some idea which sites were likely to be among the earliest of their type.

It might seem that, after more than a century of interest in, and intensive study of, the archaeological remains of the British Isles, few new sites remain to be recognised. This is true of many areas, particularly of those which are now densely populated or which have been farming land for several centuries. It is not true of many upland areas, for example in Scotland, or in areas which are not today considered as good farming land, as in the west of Ireland. During the past few years many hitherto unrecognised prehistoric sites have been discovered, sites which we can now see are obviously the remains of structures and which in several cases lie no more than a few yards from roads in frequent use for centuries. Some such sites have been recognised by full-time archaeologists. Others have been discovered by a variety of people, particularly by local archaeologists who were familiar with their own areas and who were quick to identify in the field features of archaeological significance.

Although it is unlikely that a site as spectacular as Altamira or Lascaux remains to be discovered in Britain or Ireland, it is not impossible that many sites of considerable archaeological value remain to be identified. It is even more probable that many, many small objects of archaeological importance are likely to be found. For various reasons, by natural agencies and because of human activity, such finds may occur in many areas at almost any time. We have only to consult archaeological periodicals to realise how many casual finds are made each year, and many of these by young people.   We shall never know how many similar finds are made, but are not recognised and are therefore lost.   In this book we shall learn to recognise and to record.

CHAPTER II

Maps and Aerial Photographs

MAPS are of great importance in all archaeological studies. The map is one of the most useful tools of the field archaeologist, both in the field and indoors. In this chapter we shall examine the advantages for the archaeologist of the different Ordnance Survey maps published in Britain and Ireland and the use of Grid References. We shall also discuss the importance of distribution maps, the specialised archaeological maps which are published from time to time and aerial photographs.

SCALES AND THEIR RELATIVE ADVANTAGES

Maps are usually fascinating in their own right, but in the British Isles they have a more particular fascination for archaeologists. Maps published by the Ordnance Survey in Britain and Ireland have for more than a century recorded archaeological sites, and these maps are rightly the envy of countries not similarly served. Many maps published by private companies also include important archaeological sites, but in this chapter we shall restrict discussion to those published by the Ordnance Survey, as they include different types, some of which have particular relevance in archaeological field work.

One immediate and obvious use of maps is to enable

us to find particular places.   For example, if we wish
to know the position of Stonehenge we may consult a
map.   That is obvious enough, but we must make sure
to consult the correct type of map for our particular
purpose.   Maps are published at different scales.   In
other words, on a large-scale map one square inch will
represent a smaller area on the ground than it will on
a small-scale map.   We can make use of this variety of
maps, and those which are likely to be of the greatest
general value in Britain are the quarter-inch, the one-
inch and the $2\frac{1}{2}$-inch Ordnance Survey maps.   One
inch on the *one-inch map* represents one mile on the
ground.   The *quarter-inch map* is so-called because one
mile on the ground is represented by one-quarter of an
inch on the map.   One mile on the ground is represented by $2\frac{1}{2}$ inches on the $2\frac{1}{2}$-*inch map*.

How may these three types of map best be used by
field archaeologists?   Let us look at the position of
Stonehenge, as it is represented on each.   Plate I
reproduces a very small area of the relevant maps.
Because of its great importance Stonehenge is marked
on the quarter-inch map, and even the small area
shown here also includes the position of several main
roads, villages and the town of Amesbury.   This scale
is ideal if we are trying to locate a site and to find a route
to it from some distance away.   If we consult the
complete sheet (which is quarter-inch sheet 16 (Southern England)) we will see that it covers a large area
from Exeter in the south-west to Portsmouth in the south-
east and from Aberdare in the north-west to Oxford in
the north-east.   The whole of Britain is covered by
seventeen sheets, and similar maps are available for
Ireland.

It is quite easy to find Stonehenge by using the
quarter-inch map, as the site is clearly marked as lying

in the fork of a V-shaped road junction. Very few
archaeological sites, however, are marked on maps of
this scale. Many more are indicated on the one-inch
map, as may be seen on the small area reproduced at
Plate I B. Immediately we can see the general position, not only of Stonehenge but also of numbers of
burial mounds (here referred to as *tumuli*). More detail
is also given of minor roads and footpaths, so that the
position of archaeological sites in relation to modern
features is more clearly defined and their location on
the ground made easier. The complete sheet (which is
one-inch sheet 167 (Salisbury)) covers an area of about
675 square miles and, as it covers part of one of the
richest archaeological areas of Britain, many archaeological sites are marked. The whole of Britain from
the Shetlands to the Scillies is covered by 190 sheets, and
a similar series has been published for Ireland. It
would not be difficult to locate most of these sites from
the one-inch map, particularly when they lie alongside
roads, footpaths, woods or streams.

Frequently, however, it is difficult to locate sites,
even when they are marked on the one-inch map. This
is particularly true of small sites which today lie in
farming country and which may be partially concealed
by hedges or field walls. Use of the $2\frac{1}{2}$-inch map avoids
most of these difficulties. Looking at the position of
Stonehenge on the portion of the $2\frac{1}{2}$-inch reproduced
at Plate I C we can see that, in addition to the information provided on the one-inch map, field boundaries
and minor footpaths are shown. Once the appropriate
field has been identified on the ground, it is simple to
find even small sites. In more open country, where
field boundaries are few, sufficient detail, natural and
artificial, is normally shown for the position of sites
marked on the map to be located in the field. Because

of the large scale, each 2½-inch sheet covers a small area, exactly 100 square kilometres or about 38·56 square miles, and several hundreds of sheets are needed to cover Britain. At present 2½-inch maps are not published for Ireland, but similar detail is shown on six-inch Irish Ordnance Survey maps, on which one mile on the ground is represented by six inches on the map. Obviously one square inch on a six-inch sheet will represent considerably less than half the area on the ground which is represented on a 2½-inch sheet, and so more than twice as many six-inch sheets would be required to cover the same area of ground as would be covered by 2½-inch sheets. Six-inch Ordnance Survey maps are available for Britain, but as identical detail is shown at the smaller scale of 2½-inches to the mile, maps at the latter scale are normally preferable for use in the field.

Every archaeologist should aim to build up a small collection of maps for his own use. Many Public Libraries have collections of Ordnance Survey maps which may be consulted and sometimes borrowed. The young field archaeologist is likely to have the greatest interest in his own part of the British Isles, and he should therefore try to have his own copies of, at least, the one-inch and quarter-inch sheets which cover his home area. Some will be unlucky, in that their home may lie near the edge of a sheet, and may therefore need two adjoining sheets, but they will have the advantage of greater map coverage! The archaeologist in Wales is fortunate, as there is a most attractive quarter-inch sheet covering the whole Principality and the Welsh Marches. The Manxman is similarly fortunate, in that a single one-inch sheet covers the whole of his island. Ordnance Survey maps are very good value for money and, given relatively careful treatment, will survive frequent use in the field and indoors for many years. The author has found no particular advantage in buying maps mounted on cloth. Ordinary paper maps are quite adequate, and it is probably preferable to replace the cheaper paper map than to buy the more expensive cloth-mounted map, which, unless it is sectioned, is liable to wear at the same rate, particularly along the folds, as the paper map.

With the appropriate quarter-inch and one-inch sheets of his area, the archaeologist has some of the basic equipment necessary for field work. The quarter-inch map will enable him to find his way about quite a large area, either by public transport, car or bicycle. The one-inch map will mark many of the more prominent archaeological sites. If it seems likely that there may be difficulty in locating particular sites, then either six-inch or $2\frac{1}{2}$-inch maps may be consulted in libraries. A rough copy of a small area of the large-scale map may then be made, showing field boundaries or other modern features useful for identification. The sketch map should also show some easily defined major feature, which is also marked on the one-inch map, to allow correlation between the two.

One's own maps should be used sensibly. They should be considered expendable and not in the same category as books. Maps may be replaced when they wear out, which is not likely to occur until after several years of use. A map is of much more value to a field worker if he feels free to write on it either in the field or indoors. He will probably find that many more archaeological sites are marked on the $2\frac{1}{2}$-inch or six-inch maps than are shown on his one-inch map, and he will probably wish to note their position on the latter. New discoveries may also be noted. He may be interested in a particular type of site, if it occurs in his part of the country, and he may wish to mark their position prominently on his quarter-inch map. Useful additions such as these, and notes possibly made from time to time in the margin, should be transferred as neatly as possible, preferably using drawing ink, on to any replacement sheet.

So far we have been looking at the importance of maps in general and how to use them to the best advantage in locating known sites marked on the maps. Before discussing other uses we must examine the methods used by the British Ordnance Survey to mark known archaeological sites on their published maps. *Stonehenge* is printed in a distinctive manner on each of the three maps shown at Plate I. The very appearance of this type face suggests antiquity and two similar scripts are used. The first employs 𝔒𝔩𝔡 𝔈𝔫𝔤𝔩𝔦𝔰𝔥 𝔠𝔥𝔞𝔯𝔞𝔠𝔱𝔢𝔯𝔰 to denote prehistoric antiquities and the second uses 𝔊𝔢𝔯𝔪𝔞𝔫 𝔱𝔢𝔵𝔱 to mark antiquities dating from the end of the Roman period to A.D. 1688. At first glance there might appear to be little difference between these two type faces, but familiarity in using maps in the field will soon enable a distinction to be drawn. In any case, the name or description of the site, such as *tumulus* or *castle*, will normally give an indication whether an antiquity is pre- or post-Roman in date. Antiquities of the Roman period are marked in simple capital letters as, for example, VILLA or ROMAN ROAD. Many sites have local names, such as *Hetty Pegler's Tump* and *Giant's Grave*, and these are normally also included on Ordnance Survey maps. On Irish Ordnance Surveys antiquities are usually indicated in type similar to the Old English characters used on British maps.

To acquire experience of field work and the use of maps, and perhaps to serve as the basis of further original work, the young field archaeologist may gainfully begin by visiting each of the antiquities marked on the local sheet or sheets of his one-inch map. The number of antiquities will vary, but there is hardly an area in Britain, consisting of farming country, built-up areas or moorland, which does not include some antiquities. In Ireland there is scarcely a townland without its antiquities. A second stage would be to consult the six-inch or $2\frac{1}{2}$-inch sheets of the area covered by the one-inch sheet and to visit any additional sites marked. Some six-inch and $2\frac{1}{2}$-inch sheets give the find-spots of certain small finds, such as pottery or metal tools and weapons. A note should be made of any such information.

Eventually the field archaeologist may come across some new information, either a structure or a small find. We shall examine later on in this book the recognition of such things, but while we are discussing the use of maps it is convenient to examine the method of recording new information on maps. If we wish to give directions how to reach our house we usually refer to various roads and turnings ('the first on the left') and prominent landmarks ('just opposite the Post Office'). This is adequate enough in conversation, but rather cumbersome in writing. There is, however, a simple system of defining the position of any site or object on a map using letters and figures. This system should be mastered, as nowadays we frequently encounter mention of 'grid references'.

THE NATIONAL GRID AND REFERENCE SYSTEM

There are separate systems for Britain and Ireland, but the basic principle is common to both. A grid or system of horizontal and vertical lines is now printed on all Ordnance Survey maps. The distance between adjacent lines represents a fixed distance on the ground and therefore varies according to the scale of the map. On the quarter-inch map the grid lines are spaced 4 centimetres apart, representing 10 kilometres on the ground, and the squares of the grid are usually referred to as *10-kilometre squares*. On both the one-inch and the 2½-inch maps the distance between adjacent lines represents a distance on the ground of one kilometre and we speak of *kilometre squares*. These kilometre and 10-kilometre squares are in fact subdivisions of larger *100-kilometre squares*, each of which is given either a code letter (in Ireland A, B, C, etc.) or two code letters (in Britain NA, NB, NC, etc.). A sketch map of either Britain or Ireland with the relevant 100-kilometre squares and their code letters are printed for easy reference on the inside cover of folded maps. The two-letter code system of British maps replaced an earlier system which employed two figures and, for the area north of the Scottish mainland, the letter N with two figures. Some Ordnance Survey sheets may still be on sale which give both the numerical and the letter code for 100-kilometre squares.

We have seen that each 100-kilometre square is divided by grid lines into 10-kilometre squares on the quarter-inch map and into one-kilometre squares on both the one-inch and 2½-inch maps. In the margin of the 2½-inch sheet each kilometre square is further subdivided into ten divisions, each representing a distance of 100 metres on the ground. From all this we are able to give a grid reference expressed in terms of the code letters for the 100-kilometre square and the position within that square, expressed in figures, of whatever is to be recorded.

To determine the latter measurements are taken in relation to the bottom left-hand corner of the 100-kilometre square.   This diagram illustrates the method.

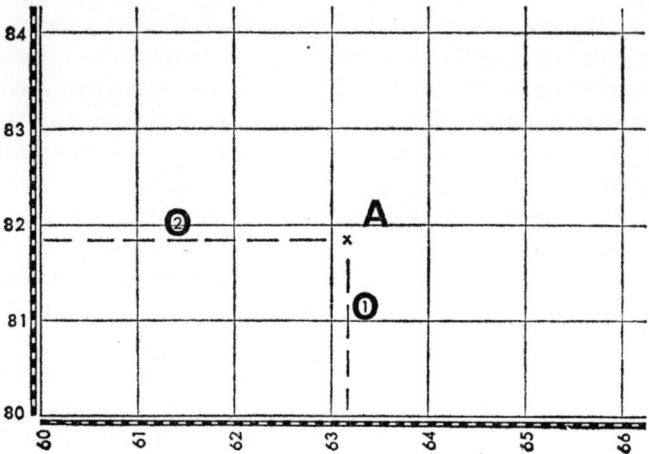

Fig. 1.

Part of a typical grid with one-kilometre squares is shown schematically, the heavier lines, as on one-inch maps, marking 100-kilometre squares.   To give the grid reference of position A we first take the left (western) edge of the kilometre square on which the position occurs and read off the two large figures printed opposite to it on the upper or lower (northern or southern) margins of the map—in this case 63.   We then estimate how many tenths to the right of that line is position A—i.e. 2.   The tenths are, of course, estimated as a fraction of the distance between adjacent grid lines.   The figure 2 is written after 63, giving 632.   Readings such as these are called *eastings*, that is the distance east of a fixed position on the grid.   Next, the *northings* must be read from the map.   To do this we take the bottom (southern) edge of the square in which position A lies and read off the two large figures printed opposite that line on the left or right (western or eastern) margins of the map—81. Estimate tenths northwards—8, and so our northings are 818. The full grid reference, correct to 100 metres, of position A is therefore 632818. This is called a *six-figure grid reference*. We must always remember to give eastings first, followed by northings, otherwise there will be much confusion.

What such a grid reference is telling in a most precise and economical manner is that position A is 63·2 kilometres (63 kilometres, 200 metres) east and 81·8 kilometres (81 kilometres, 800 metres) north of the south-western (bottom left-hand) corner of a 100-kilometre square. It follows that the same reading will occur in each 100-kilometre square on the grid. To determine which 100-kilometre square is referred to, we quote the appropriate code letter or letters. This might be, for example, H in Ireland or NC in Britain, giving H 632818 and NC 632818 respectively. Such a grid reference is unique, that is only one position within the respective grid systems have the reference quoted.

Grid references may be applied to maps of any scale, provided that grid lines are printed on them. In giving references for use on larger-scale maps it is possible to use eight-figure grid references, so enabling greater precision in plotting positions on such maps. This is facilitated by wider spacing of grid lines on the maps and by the use of subdivisions of the grid interval on the margins of each sheet. On quarter-inch sheets single large figures only are printed in the margins, and we should normally use four-figure grid references in using such maps, although six- and eight-figure grid references may be plotted on to the map. It would not be possible, however, to give anything more accurate than a four-figure reference in reading from a quarter-inch map.

On British Ordnance Survey maps the grid system has an additional advantage. If we wish to know the number of the quarter-inch and one-inch sheet covering a particular area we may quite easily find out by reference to the cover of any map of those two scales, where an outline map of Britain is overprinted by the boundaries of each map sheet and its appropriate number. Because of the small area covered by each $2\frac{1}{2}$-inch sheet such a simple index cannot be used. As we have seen, each $2\frac{1}{2}$-inch sheet covers a 10-kilometre square of the National Grid. The quarter-inch map has a grid of 10-kilometre squares only, so that each sheet provides a ready index for $2\frac{1}{2}$-inch sheets of that area. To determine the number of any particular $2\frac{1}{2}$-inch sheet (which is expressed in terms of the National Grid) we take the reading of the south-western corner and give the code letters of the appropriate 100-kilometre grid. A two-figure reference is adequate, so that we read only the large figures printed in the margins. A six-figure reference would read, for example, 300500, but the noughts are superfluous, so we would use 35, preceded by the code letters, for example SJ 35. On the one-inch map 10-kilometre squares are also printed in heavy lines, so that the same principle may be used.

DISTRIBUTION MAPS

We have already spoken of the importance of plotting new discoveries on to maps, and this is an important aspect of recording. Archaeology, however, consists of more than the mere collection of objects and facts,

and maps are of considerable value in the interpretation
of such facts.   Archaeological cultures (see above, page
14) have two boundaries.   One is a time boundary,
in that all objects and sites of any culture must have
been in use at about the same time.   Cultures also
have geographical boundaries, as the component parts
of a culture exist within a specific area.   Such an area

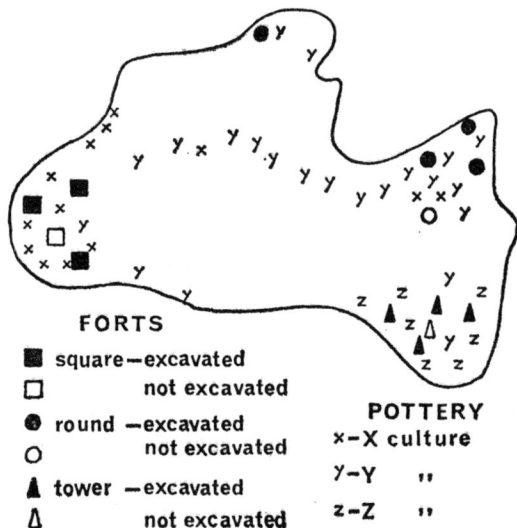

FORTS

■ square—excavated

□   not excavated

● round —excavated

○   not excavated

▲ tower —excavated

△   not excavated

POTTERY

x—X culture

y—Y   ,,

z—Z   ,,

Fig. 2.

is most readily defined by plotting find spots and
structures on to a simple outline map.

Fig. 2 is an outline map of an imaginary island,
which we will call *Inis*.   On it are plotted the positions
of three types of pottery (also imaginary), marked
respectively *x*, *y* and *z*, and three types of structure,
symbols differentiating between excavated and unexcavated sites.   It is assumed that all are contemporary.
Study of the map reveals several facts.   The pottery of

the three cultures (which we may call respectively the X, Y and Z Cultures) is concentrated mainly within well-defined boundaries. Finds of the Z Culture are not known beyond the south-eastern corner of the island, but finds of the X Culture, while primarily concentrated in the south-west, are known also from the distribution area of the Y Culture, although not in that of the Z Culture. The Y Culture also has a well-defined distribution area in the eastern part of Inis, but its pottery is also found not only in the other distribution areas but also scattered throughout the island. Each of the three types of structure also has a well-defined distribution. Square forts and towers are concentrated respectively in the south-west and south-east of the island, and belong respectively to the X and Z Cultures. In an actual archaeological context the appropriate pottery would probably have been found in most of the excavated structures. Round forts have a wider distribution, similar to that of Y pottery, although they are not found in the distribution area of the other two types.

Certain interpretations are suggested. The X and Y Cultures appear to have been in trade contact with each other along a well-defined route, judging by the occurrence of small numbers of pots in each other's territory, but the Z Culture appears to have been unable or unwilling to export. No single culture dominated either of the other two, although the Y Culture appears to have begun to expand along the north coast of the island.

All this may appear to be self-evident, but a distribution map presents pictorially, economically and quite simply a considerable body of evidence. Our example is very elementary, but more detailed maps follow the same general principles. Where a considerable body of facts is to be recorded it is generally preferable to draw two or more separate maps, each recording a proportion of the whole. To return to Inis, we find that there are other structures and tools which can be shown to be contemporary with the information plotted on Fig. 2. Again, certain distribution patterns emerge, and this enables us to give greater precision in defining the cultural content. The X Culture had square forts, buried its dead in stone tombs, used copper daggers and its distinctive pottery. The Y Culture had towers but no known type of burial structure, used stone battle-axes and its own pottery. The Z Culture had round forts, buried its dead in pit-graves, used the bow and arrow (inferred from the existence of bronze arrow-heads) and also its own pottery (Figs. 3 and 4).

It must not be assumed, of course, that our interpretation of cultural content is based exclusively on distribution maps, but they do provide an important basis for the definition of geographical limits for cultures. Distribution maps are frequently drawn and

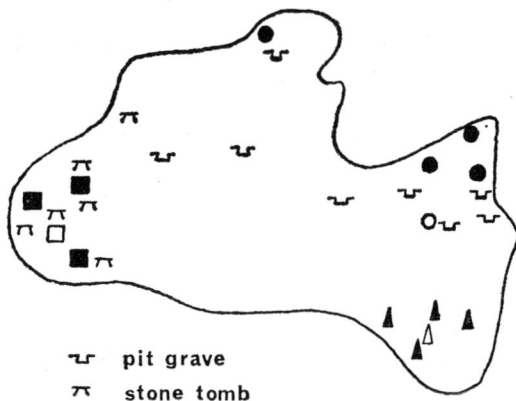

Fig. 3.

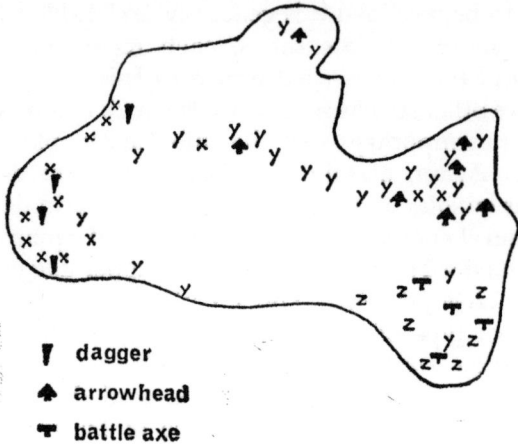

I dagger

♠ arrowhead

T battle axe

Fig. 4.

redrawn as new evidence is discovered or as earlier evidence is modified.

ORDNANCE SURVEY PERIOD MAPS

During the past forty years the Ordnance Survey in Britain has published a number of *period maps* on which the antiquities of certain periods are plotted on different backgrounds. The *Map of Ancient Britain* gives the position of the more important visible antiquities of Britain dating from before A.D. 1066. Each site is named, and symbols are used to differentiate between sites of different periods. These are plotted on a lightly printed map of modern Britain at a scale of about 10 miles to 1 inch, showing towns and villages, roads, railways, rivers and high ground. An index is available and classifies the sites, gives a six-figure grid reference and the number of the relevant one-inch Ordnance Survey sheet. All sites plotted on the *Map of Ancient Britain* also appear on the one-inch series. *Ancient Britain* is published in two sheets, the division between the north and south sheets coming at a line drawn through the Lake District and the North York Moors. The map is useful in that it lists important visible sites and provides grid references. It might be of use in the early stages of making a local study of field monuments, but it is essentially a tourist's map, and a most useful one in that context.

A similar background is used for the two sheets of the *Map of Monastic Britain*. This classifies and plots the position of monasteries and similar religious centres which existed in England until the reign of Henry VIII, and in Scotland until the sixteenth century. No distinction is made, either on the map or in the accompanying index, between sites of which remains are at present visible and those which are not. To a field worker concerned with Medieval Archaeology, however, the map would be of great potential value, in that the discovery of monastic remains could immediately be correlated with the written evidence and the monastery identified. A *Map of Monastic Ireland* at the same scale has been published by the Irish Ordnance Survey.

A *Map of Hadrian's Wall* is also published against a faintly printed background, but at a scale of 2 inches to 1 mile. It provides an immediate visual summary of available knowledge concerning the Wall and its associated structures. It also differentiates by its use of colour between remains which are now visible and those which are not. As the background is sufficiently detailed to include field boundaries, it is easy to locate on the ground any visible feature or the site of others no longer visible. The map is an excellent tool for the field worker interested in Roman frontier defences.

c

The *Map of Roman Britain*, now in its third edition, is of more general interest to the student of that period. The map is printed at a scale of 16 miles to 1 inch against the physical background of hills, mountains and rivers, but without reference to modern towns and communications. It includes structures, both visible and invisible, and small finds. A very full topographical index makes use of the National Grid to enable the parish and county of any structure which is plotted on the map to be identified, together with the numbers of the relevant six-inch and one-inch sheets. The $2\frac{1}{2}$-inch sheet number may be determined from the grid reference. A considerable body of supplementary detail, including additional maps, is given in the introduction. The *Map of Southern Britain in the Iron Age*, printed at a scale of about 10 miles to the inch, deals in a comparable manner with the period and area indicated by its title. The *Map of Britain in the Dark Ages* was published some time ago and, although it is not up to date, it remains of value to field workers.

In addition, the Ordnance Survey published a series of period maps at a scale of 4 miles to 1 inch, using the basic quarter-inch map as a background. These were really specialised distribution maps of Neolithic structures in the Cotswolds, south-eastern England, the Trent Basin and Wessex. Although they are not up to date, nor are they generally available for sale, except perhaps occasionally in second-hand book shops, they are still of value and may be consulted in certain libraries.

The more recently published period maps, particularly those dealing with Roman and Iron Age Britain, are highly sophisticated examples of distribution maps. With the use of coloured symbols a great body of evidence is conveniently assembled. Archaeologists may use this information to further their own field work. The index and its use of grid references allow easy transference to large-scale maps, which may be used in the field.   It is of interest to realise that much of the information plotted on such maps has been provided by local archaeologists, some of them young people.

AERIAL PHOTOGRAPHS

Although we are concerned in this book only with the recognition of sites which are today visible at ground level, it is important to realise that traces of ancient structures which are invisible on the ground may be seen from the air.   A site may be completely levelled so that there are no irregularities on the ground surface, but it is difficult to obliterate completely all evidence of Man's past disturbance of the earth.   If a ditch has been dug and allowed to fill up again naturally, a slight hollow will be visible on the ground surface.   If, however, the area has been ploughed over a number of years, the action of the plough will spread the soil so that any remains of a mound or ditch will be destroyed and will merge into a level surface.   Despite this, the digging of a ditch disturbs the subsoil and may affect the growth of crops immediately above the line of the ditch for many centuries after surface indications have disappeared.

As the subsoil has been disturbed along the line of the ditch, it is looser than that of the surrounding area. The roots of crops growing over the former ditch can penetrate farther than those of the surrounding crops. The former produces a stronger growth which is taller than that surrounding it.   It also takes a little longer to ripen, so that from the air the position of a buried ditch or pit will often show as a green area in a field of ripening corn. The period when these colour changes, or *crop marks*, are visible is usually short, perhaps restricted to a few days in summer. Crop marks may not be visible every year, particularly in excessively dry or excessively wet summers. When crop marks do appear, they may reveal the position of ploughed-out round barrows, ritual sites, grain-storage pits, defensive earthworks and even timber-built structures. Roman or other buildings with buried stone foundations may also be revealed from aerial photographs, as buried remains prevent roots of crops from penetrating as far as those in the surrounding area. In this case the crop growing over the buried feature is weaker and ripens more rapidly than the surrounding crop. It shows up from the air as lighter-coloured markings against a darker background.

The aerial photograph merely records what the eye can see from an aeroplane, and it is clearly more convenient to study a photograph than to examine a site by circling above it. Many important sites have been discovered from the air, and more are found each year. The latter are now usually located during flights arranged specially for the purpose. Sites may also be recognised on aerial photographs taken some time ago for other purposes. These include series of photographs taken by the Royal Air Force which cover the whole of Britain. Copies of photographs covering local areas are sometimes held by Public Libraries. A field archaeologist making a detailed survey of local antiquities should consult all available aerial photographs. The local librarian or museum curator should be able to help in locating the nearest available collection of photographs.

CHAPTER III

The Physical Background

In the last chapter we saw that certain period maps published by the Ordnance Survey include physical features, such as rivers and high ground. This may be seen on the maps of the Iron Age and Roman Britain. An earlier edition of the latter attempted to reconstruct a map of the vegetation as it was in Roman times. This emphasises the necessity of studying all evidence which has a bearing on the past. Sites and small finds cannot be studied in isolation. They must constantly be related to the physical background. If the physical background of the time in question can be reconstructed so much the better. If not, we have to attempt to draw whatever conclusions seem valid from a study of the present environment. An Historian—or an Industrial Archaeologist—studying the origins of the Industrial Revolution would need to take into account the location of coal and iron in order to write a balanced account. Even in the prehistoric period the proximity or absence of certain raw materials affected the development of local cultures. In an age before the widespread use of efficient tools the environment might also influence in varying degrees both the pattern of settlement and the economy.

If we return to our imaginary island, Inis, and its archaeology and now plot our finds against the physical background the whole map becomes more meaningful. When we add the high ground, rivers and marshes, certain features begin to make more sense (Fig. 5). For simplicity, the symbols x, y and z are used to mark both structures and small finds. Very high ground is likely to deter movement, particularly when it rises steeply, as we may assume it did in the ridge between Culture Y and Z. We may also assume,

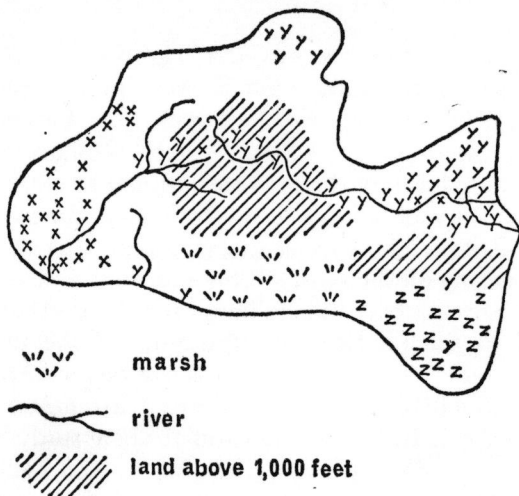

marsh

river

land above 1,000 feet

Fig. 5.

and this would be shown by contour lines on a large-scale map, that the central upland mass rises gently from the east and more steeply from the west. This would help to explain why it was that the Y Culture rather than the X Culture appears to have pioneered contact between the two culture areas. Marshes would also have inhibited settlement and communication. On Inis it helps to explain why the Z Culture seems to have been so hemmed in. Rivers, on the other hand, may encourage and assist communications, and the main route across the island was by rivers.

We must not assume that physical factors such as these actually determined choice of settlement. It must always be allowed that Man had a free choice. He *could* have lived on the mountain-tops or in the marshes of Inis, but he may have found it difficult and dangerous. The field archaeologist must take into account physical features not only in looking for new sites in particular areas but also in interpreting his evidence.

Features such as rivers, mountains and marshes are readily recognised, and the influence they may have exerted in choice of settlement in prehistoric times is fairly obvious. Other physical features are initially less apparent, but their influence was no less important. In the prehistoric period in the British Isles poorly drained soils generally tended to limit settlement. Such soils would normally have carried fairly heavy forest cover and dense undergrowth. Trees could have been felled and undergrowth cleared, but the soil would have been too heavy to till with limited equipment, which did not include the plough until the middle of the Bronze Age. Lighter, naturally drained soils were preferred, particularly chalk and gravel. Some light soils, such as sand, were avoided by early farmers as being too acidic, although they did attract Mesolithic hunters.

We may now relate our distribution map to a simplified soil map (Fig. 6). The marshy area in the south of the island obviously had poor drainage, as has the river valley to the east of the X Culture. This might partially explain the lack of eastwards expansion of that culture and its tendency to spread along the north-west coast. The mountainous ridge between the Y and Z Cultures is also badly drained, but the large central upland mass has well-drained soil. Altitude and rainfall, and possibly acidity of soil, would tend to limit settlement of a farming people. Study of an actual area which reproduced conditions similar to those of the imaginary Inis might reveal evidence that the central upland area had been occupied at the same time by hunting peoples, but that little other than casual surface finds had been made on the badly drained upland ridge.

Within the relatively small geographical area of the

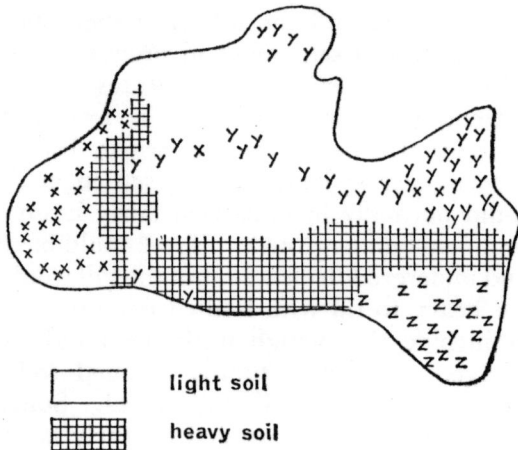

light soil

heavy soil

Fig. 6.

British Isles there is abundant variety of scenery, mountain and lowland, forest and moorland, lakes and rivers, indented coastline and islands, valleys and plains. Much of this scenery has been modified by human activity during the past 5,000 years, from the time when Neolithic farmers initiated the long process of change which has led to our present diversified landscape. Forests have been cleared, marshland has been drained to provide land for farming. The diversity of the natural environment has further been enhanced by the variety of *vernacular architecture*, that is cottages and small houses. In the midlands of England and in part of the south-east we find that traditional architecture makes use of brick, often in conjunction with half-timbering. In East Anglia flint gives a distinctive appearance to vernacular architecture. From the Neolithic period onwards the particular properties of Cotswold oolite and Caithness flagstone were appreciated, and both areas produced a distinctive architectural tradition. In the Highlands of Scotland, in many parts of Wales and Ireland, stone-built cottages give those countries much of their scenic flavour. In the same way, field boundaries mirror the local environment. The rich farming areas of the English midlands have their hedges, whereas in the upland areas we find extensive use of dry-stone walls. The larger houses were less dependent on local materials in building, as their owners could afford to have stone brought in from some distance away. This process began in the Roman period, although the transport of large quantities of building stone was not unknown in prehistoric times. In the prehistoric period, too, wood was used extensively for building in those areas where it was plentiful.

The field archaeologist must be aware of the several factors which have influenced building traditions in the British Isles from the Neolithic onwards. These factors are dependent on the solid geology of the different regions, and as soon as we compare a distribution map of prehistoric stone monuments with a geological map we can appreciate the reason why these are to be found in western and northern Britain and in Ireland. To oversimplify, if we wish to attempt to discover hitherto unrecognised stone monuments we should not seek them in the clay lowlands of central England.

The Geological Surveys of Great Britain and Ireland each publish geological maps printed on outline maps of the Ordnance Survey. Britain is covered by two sheets at a scale of 10 miles to 1 inch, and these should frequently be consulted to gain a general geological appreciation of the area being studied. They will frequently be of assistance in understanding distribution patterns of particular types of monument. More detailed maps at a scale of one mile to one inch are also published for Britain and Ireland, and these, too, should be consulted for more detailed studies. Many Public Libraries have collections of the geological maps of their districts.

Appreciation of solid geology may also be relevant in assessing the significance of casual finds. For most of the prehistoric period stone, particularly flint, was the most important raw material used in the manufacture of tools and weapons. Flint, for example, had to be imported into a non-flint-bearing area, and even a casual find of a flint tool or weapon has an added significance if it is found some distance away from the nearest source of flint. Even the waste products of flint working, if found casually in any quantity on the ground surface, may provide a lead to the eventual recognition of a prehistoric habitation or camping site. Axes were also made of fine, hard-grained rock, which in their natural state occur mainly in the upland areas of western and northern Britain and in Ireland. Such axes are frequently found in lowland Britain, and even casual finds are of value in assessing the volume and extent of prehistoric trade, both in the raw material and the finished object.

It must be emphasised that factors such as soil, altitude, rainfall and geology did not determine either choice of settlement or a way of life. They did influence—and still influence—cultural development, and the field archaeologist must always be aware of the possible influence factors such as these had on local development, particularly in the prehistoric period.

CHAPTER IV

Field Monuments

CAIRNS AND STANDING STONES

WE now turn to the material remains of the past, and in this and the following chapters we shall examine the more important types of field monument and small finds in Britain and Ireland. In these chapters each type will be discussed as far as possible in chronological order.

In describing stone structures a limit is set on those of prehistoric and early historic date. Properly speaking, the study of medieval castles and churches is the concern of the archaeologist, but this is a specialised study and is normally dealt with in books on Architecture. Reference to books on this subject is made in the section on further reading (see below, page 204). Once we begin to examine pre-medieval stone structures we find a preponderance of ritual and fortified sites and relatively few visible remains of domestic structures of any great size. In this the prehistoric period resembles the Middle Ages, as in both periods houses were not built to last for any length of time. Ritual sites were intended to last, and in both periods there is evidence of rebuilding and reconstruction. Fortified sites similarly had to be strongly built, whether they were medieval castles or Iron Age hill-forts, and accordingly, their strong construction has contributed to their survival.

BURIAL MOUNDS—CHAMBERED CAIRNS

Remains of several hundred stone-built burial mounds containing internal structures survive in Britain and Ireland. It is not possible to give an accurate figure of their number, and this is an indication of the continuing need for intensive field work. It is probable, however, that in England and Wales there are probably some 300 sites, in Scotland perhaps 600 or more, and in Ireland at least 1,200. Although there are many varieties of plan, they fall into more or less well-defined geographical and cultural groups, and we shall look at these in turn. Before doing so, some of the terms used in megalithic studies may be examined.

The word *megalithic* means simply, 'of big stones', and refers to the frequent use of large stone slabs in construction. A *chambered cairn* is a burial mound containing a stone-built chamber, in which bodies were placed, and which was covered by an enclosing cairn built of smaller stones. Such structures are frequently called *megalithic tombs*, but this description should be applied only when the chamber is built of large slabs and not when the chamber is built solely of dry-stone walling. The term 'megalith' is often used incorrectly to refer to a chambered cairn, and this should be avoided. *Megalith* means 'large stone', and may refer either to a single standing stone or to one of several large slabs used in a variety of structures, not exclusively chambered cairns. We should also distinguish between cairn and barrow. A *cairn* is a stone-built mound and a *barrow* one built of earth or of earth and turf (sods).

In a burial chamber of megalithic construction the side walls are usually built of *orthostats*, that is, large stones forming an essential part of the structure. An orthostat is to be distinguished from a *menhir*, which is also a megalith, but which is free-standing and does not form part of a composite structure. Menhirs are sometimes found in isolation (see below, page 77) and sometimes near the entrance to chambered cairns.

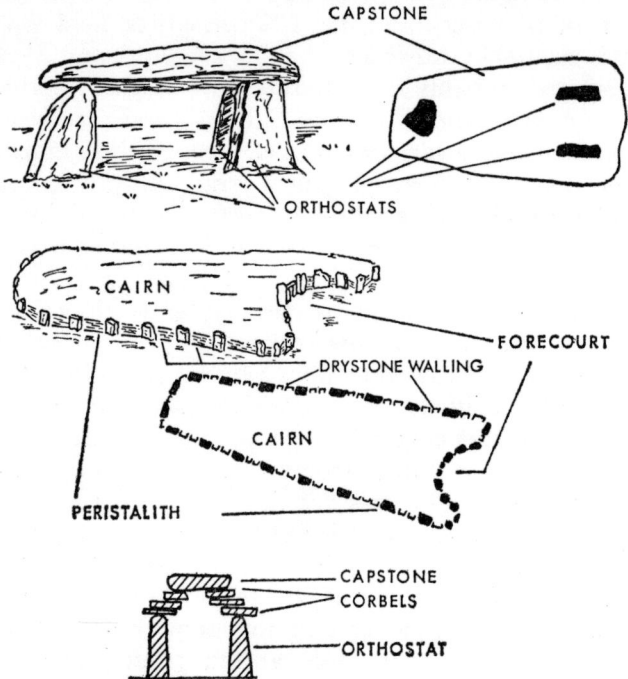

Fig. 7.

In the latter case they are not in direct physical contact with the remainder of the structure. A burial chamber may also be of *dry-stone* construction, of flat stones laid on top of each other without the use of mortar. Orthostats and dry-stone walling were frequently used in conjunction with each other (Fig. 7).

Excavation has shown that the cairn covering the chamber was often composed of several structural components, sometimes delimited by internal stone walls, but it is exceptional to be able to identify such structures in field survey. It is sometimes possible in field work to recognise cairns that were of more than one period of construction. The structure of medieval churches and cathedrals was frequently altered and, in the same way, excavation has shown that additional structures were sometimes built on to existing chambered cairns, which hitherto had been complete in themselves. A cairn of round plan, for example, might be altered by the addition of extra cairn material into one with a long plan. This additional material might or might not include additional chambered structures. On the ground it is sometimes possible to identify the junction between the two parts in the form of a shallow depression in the body of the mound.

The limits of a cairn are often marked either by a kerb of dry-stone walling or by a *peristalith* of small upright stones, sometimes by both (Fig. 7). On account of movement of cairn material, both natural and because of later human disturbance, it is rarely possible without excavation to identify precisely the original limits of the cairn. Tops of the small stones of the peristalith and short stretches of dry-stone walling may be visible. The plan of the cairn proper after excavation will often differ from that visible before excavation on account of *slip* of cairn material from the body of the mound. This slip is sometimes referred to as *extra-revetment material*. A dry-stone wall enclosing the body of a cairn is also known as a *revetment*. Despite this, it is normally possible to determine without excavation whether a cairn is round or long in plan. Of course, in a number of cases all cairn material had been removed and only part of the chamber structure survives. It will be appreciated that a large cairn, perhaps containing several thousand tons of easily moved stone would have been attractive to farmers in more recent times as a source of stone for the building of field walls and farm buildings.   Field walls are often found near to denuded

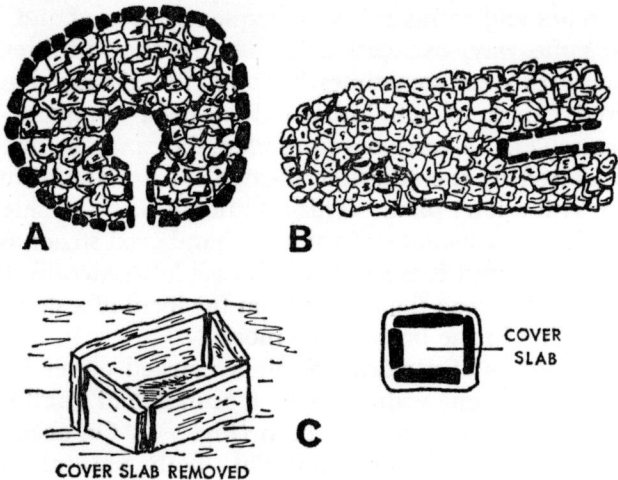

Fig. 8.

cairns, and it is obvious that such cairns were robbed to provide stone.

We have referred to round cairns and long cairns. These are the two most common plans found in Britain and Ireland.   There are certain more specialised types, which are discussed below, but these are merely variants of the two major types.   The plan of the chamber varies among different groups, but there are again two main types, the passage grave and the gallery grave.   In the *passage grave* a distinction is made between the chamber proper, of varying shape but usually round or polygonal in plan, and the entrance passage which may vary in length (Fig. 8 A). In the *gallery grave* there is no formal distinction between passage and chamber. The simplest form of gallery grave is rectangular in plan (Fig. 8 B). Small side chambers, opening from the main chamber, are sometimes found in passage graves. The stone-built *cist*, a small, box-like, roofed structure containing burials, should not be confused with the chamber of a chambered cairn (Fig. 8 C). Access was provided into the latter from outside the cairn, and such burial mounds often remained in use for a number of years. They were, in a sense, family vaults and, although the entrance might be blocked after each burial, it was possible to remove the blocking and so gain access into the chamber. The cist, when enclosed in a cairn, did not have an entrance, being a closed box. It is probable that the majority of such structures were used only once, and many were then covered over by cairn material. Cists were also set in the ground, without any covering cairn.

The subdivisions of cairn and chamber plan have long provided the basis of classification, particularly as passage graves often occur in round cairns and gallery graves in long cairns. While this remains a useful concept, we should not attempt to force all chambered cairns into one or other of these categories. In the British Isles there is much variety of plan, a variety probably resulting from the coming together of peoples with differing architectural, and probably ritual, traditions.

D

THE CHAMBERED CAIRNS OF ENGLAND AND WALES

The majority of chambered cairns in England and Wales lie in the west, and we may distinguish four main geographical groups in the Scillies and Cornwall, in south-west Wales, in north-west Wales and in the Severn area. In addition, there are smaller groups in

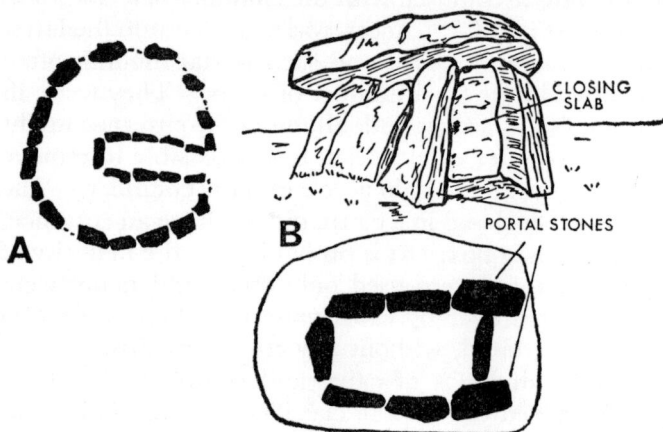

Fig. 9

the southern part of the Peak District, in the Isle of Man and in Kent. Isolated cairns have also been found in north-west England.

(a) *The Scillies and Cornwall.* The main concentration of cairns in this group is to be found in the Isles of Scilly and in Cornwall, and to them may be added a smaller scatter in Devon and Dorset. All the known cairns in the Scillies, and four in Cornwall, belong to one type of structure, sometimes referred to as *entrance graves.* The plan of the chamber is often rectangular, but sometimes the inner part is wider than the outer.

All are enclosed in circular cairns with well-built kerbs. They may vary in diameter from 10 to 75 feet, but the majority are between 20 and 40 feet (Fig. 9 A).

There is more variety of plan among the cairns of Cornwall, Devon and Dorset, but the majority of chambers are small and rectangular in plan. An important type of cairn, which is also found in Wales and Ireland, is the *portal dolmen* (Fig. 9 B). This has a small rectangular chamber, normally set within a small oval cairn. Its entrance is marked by a pair of prominent stones, *the portals*, which are often taller and more massive than the other orthostats, and because of this, many surviving portal dolmens have capstones which slope downwards from the entrance. There is often a flat closing slab between the portals. The term, *dolmen*, is often used to describe a simple rectangular or polygonal chamber which does not have a passage. Some Cornish sites might be classified as dolmens.

Both round and long cairns have been identified in this group, and at least one of the latter has an orthostatic forecourt.

(b) *South-west Wales.* This group comprises cairns in Pembrokeshire and Carmarthenshire. There is some variety in the plan of chambers. Many are simple and include portal dolmens, but a larger type of gallery grave has also been identified. Most cairns contain one chamber each, but at least one site has a number of small chambers arranged radially around the circumference of the cairn. Both long and round cairns have been identified, and at least two of the former have orthostatic forecourts.

(c) *North-west Wales.* There is also some variety of plan in cairns of this group which are found in Anglesey, Merionethshire, Caernarvonshire and Denbighshire. The portal dolmen is common. It is normally set

in a small cairn, but some appear to have been incorporated into long cairns.

Passage graves enclosed in round cairns are found in
Anglesey. Two of these, *Bryn Celli Ddu* and *Barclodiad
y Gawres*, have orthostats decorated with motives similar
to those found in some Irish passage graves (see below,
page 79). The remaining cairns in the island are less
easily classified, but appear to include polygonal dolmens, although some of these may be the remains of
passage graves. Little of the cairn survives at most of
the latter sites.

(d) *The Severn Area.* This group comprises some 150
cairns in the counties of Glamorgan, Monmouth,
Brecon, Hereford, Somerset, Gloucester, Oxford, Wiltshire and Berkshire. It forms a fairly well-defined
distribution pattern on both sides of the Severn, with a
concentration of cairns in the upland area of the Cotswolds, and may be referred to as the *Cotswold–Severn
Group*. In the past there has been a tendency to over-
emphasise the importance of the Severn as a route into
the area. It was suggested that people bringing with
them cairns of this group arrived in the Severn Estuary
by sea from north-west France and subsequently
spread inland into south-east Wales, on the one hand,
and on to the Cotswolds, on the other. More recent
study reveals that this is an oversimplified conclusion
based too exclusively on distribution. It illustrates one
possible type of error which may arise from a study of
distribution patterns alone, without reference to a
detailed study of structural plans.

The majority of cairns of the Cotswold–Severn Group
are long and straight-sided, although their original plan
may not be determined in many cases until after
excavation. Most taper from a broader, higher end,
usually facing in an easterly direction, to a lower,

narrower end, giving a trapezoidal plan. At the
broader end there is often an indentation which marks
the site of a forecourt.

Within cairns of this type there are three basic

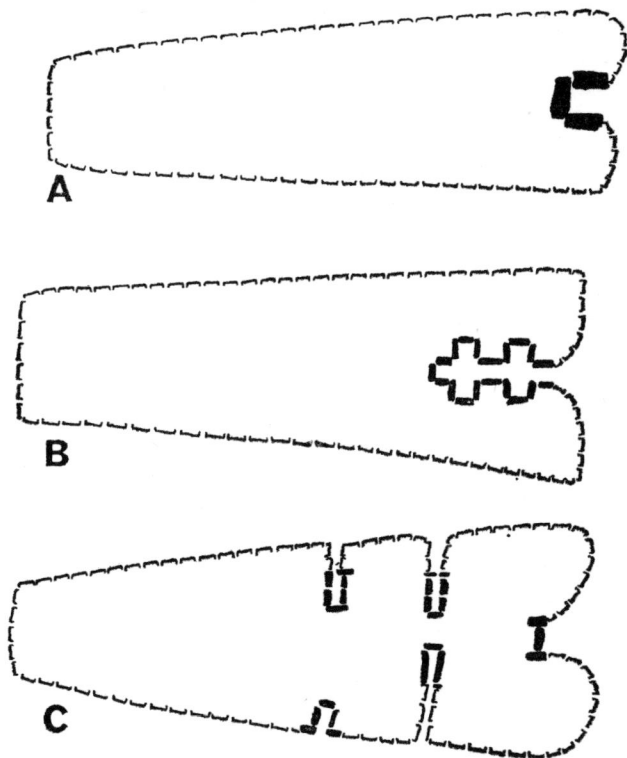

Fig. 10.

chamber plans. The first is set within the broader
end of the cairn and is a simple, square or rectangular
chamber, the sides and end-stone of which are often
built of single orthostats (Fig. 10 A). The second type,

also entered from a forecourt at the broader end, consists of a central passage, from the opposed sides of which open pairs of chambers. Because of the resemblance in plan to transepts in ecclesiastical architecture, these are usually known as *transepted chambers* (Fig. 10 B). There may be one, two, three or more pairs of transepts. These are both *terminally chambered cairns*, as the chambers are entered from the end, as opposed to the side, of the cairn.

The third type is a *laterally chambered cairn* in which one or more chambers are entered from one or both long sides of the cairn. The chamber structure normally comprises an orthostatic chamber, which is polygonal or rectangular in plan and which is approached by a passage. The latter was often built of both dry-stone walling and orthostats and was normally roofed at a lower level than the chamber (Fig. 10 C).

In some cairns orthostats were erected between the chamber and passage at right angles to the main axis of the chamber. These *jambs*, as they are termed, restricted access into the chamber. At least two cairns of this group had a porthole in a similar position. The *porthole* was formed of two jambs so positioned that their edges were in contact with each other. To allow access, semicircular hollows were cut in stone, giving a roughly circular aperture.

Although access into chambers of this class was from the long sides of the cairn, the forecourt in the broader end was retained, presumably for ritual reasons, as it had no structural or functional purpose. In several cairns a megalithic structure, resembling a doorway blocked by a flat slab, was built in the forecourt in the position occupied by the entrance in a terminally chambered cairn. Such an 'entrance' is termed a *blind entrance* or *false portal* (Fig. 11).

Each of the three types of cairn is found throughout the Cotswolds–Severn area as a whole. There are also hybrid cairns in which transepted chambers were set laterally in long cairns. It seems possible that the idea of building long, trapezoidal cairns was derived from earthen mounds of similar size and proportions which were in use at approximately the same time in the chalk areas to the east. There were separate traditions of chamber structure, each derived from different sources.

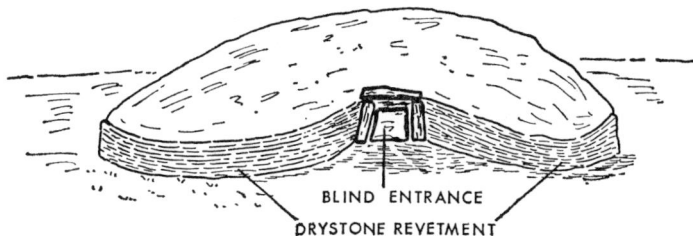

BLIND ENTRANCE
DRYSTONE REVETMENT
Fig. 11.

The tradition of building long cairns with a dry-stone revetment appears to have spread to north-west Wales and eventually to the north of Ireland and to south-west Scotland, where it influenced the local development of chambered cairns.

(e) *The Peak District.* There are seven or eight cairns in this group, one each in Cheshire and Staffordshire and the remainder in Derbyshire. Present surface indications show that there are both long and round cairns containing simple rectangular chambers and others of passage grave tradition. One long cairn has a forecourt.

(f) *The Isle of Man.* The seven or eight cairns on the island also include two long cairns with forecourt and others with rectangular chambers. There is also a unique site, *Meayll Hill*, in which six T-shaped megalithic chambered structures are arranged on the circumference of a circle, their entrances facing outwards.

(g) *Kent.* The five known sites in the Medway Valley appear to have had rectangular chambers set in long rectangular cairns. Their location contrasts markedly with the other cairns of England and Wales in their easterly position. Whereas it can be shown that the majority of cairns in the British Isles were influenced by ideas brought from the Atlantic coasts of Europe, those of Kent have their closest parallels in similar cairns in Holland and northern Germany. This conclusion may be drawn quite easily on the basis of field work alone, from a consideration of geographical position and comparison of plans of existing structures with those of northern Europe.

THE CHAMBERED CAIRNS OF SCOTLAND

The chambered cairns of Scotland may also be divided for convenience of discussion into regional groups, which also appear to reflect distinct cultural traditions. The groups are south-west Scotland, the Western Isles, northern Scotland, and the Orkneys and Shetlands.

(a) *South-west Scotland.* From its geographical position it might be assumed that south-west Scotland would have been influenced by ideas moving northwards along the Irish Sea which contributed to the development of chambered cairns in the area. Present evidence suggests that this was so, and it is possible to speak of a *Solway–Clyde group*, although current field work in the area suggests that a distinction may be made between the cairns of the Solway area and those of the Clyde region.

One of the distinctive types of cairn in south-west
Scotland is the *horned cairn*, in which the chamber is
entered through a semicircular forecourt set in the
broader end of a long cairn.   The forecourt is marked
by a *façade* of orthostats, sometimes linked by dry-stone
walling, the whole having a crescentic or semicircular

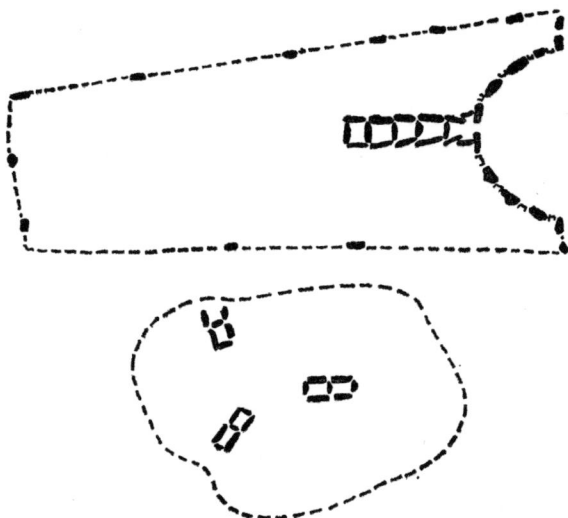

Fig. 12.

plan.   The chamber is rectangular in plan, normally
divided into *segments* by orthostats set transversely to
the main axis.   These orthostats are termed *septal slabs*
and are often as tall as or taller than the side walls.
There may be two, three, four or five segments (Fig. 12
upper).
   Some trapezoidal cairns, which often cover horned
cairns, are more than 100 feet long and their general
proportions are similar to those of the Cotswold–Severn
area.   In the absence of suitable stone, the high

standard of dry-stone walling seen in the Cotswolds is rarely apparent in south-west Scotland, but Scottish cairns often have well-built peristaliths of small uprights and dry-stone walling.

Segmented rectangular chambers enclosed in smaller, oval cairns are also known in the area (Fig. 12 *lower*). In some cairns there may be more than one chambered structure, some of which are set laterally in the cairn. A few simple rectangular chambers, or dolmens, have been identified, and it is possible that the segmented chamber was evolved locally from the idea of building additional chambers on to an existing simple chamber. The forecourt appears to have developed in the Irish Sea area, and the trapezoidal cairn may have derived from the Cotswold–Severn area.

(b) *The Western Isles*. At the time of writing there is no adequate published account of cairns in this area, although many cairns are known to exist and field work is locating more. Both long and short cairns are known, some with forecourts and some without. There are passage graves and segmented chambers, and it is apparent, both from field work and from its geographical position, that the area received influences moving northwards from southern Scotland and from Ireland.

(c) *Northern Scotland*. This is one of the most fascinating areas in the whole of Europe for the study of chambered cairns. There is variety of plan, immediately recognisable in the field, and many such plans were clearly the result of local development and cannot be paralleled precisely elsewhere in Europe. From Inverness northwards to the north coast of Scotland there appears to have been a cultural province, although within it there was much variety of cairn plan. Unlike the Cotswolds–Severn area, where

there are chambers of different plan covered by cairns
of similar plan, many of the burial mounds of northern
Scotland have a chamber of basically similar plan, but
set in cairns of varied plan.   Three main types of
cairns may be distinguished, the Camster type, the
Yarrows type and the Ormiegill type, each named from
excavated cairns in Caithness.

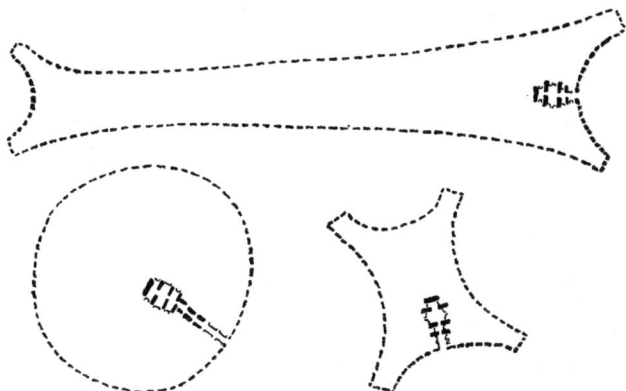

Fig. 13. *Upper:* Yarrows type.   *Lower:* Camster and Ormiegill
types.

Despite the variety of plan of surrounding cairn, the
plan of the chamber is simply a variant on the passage
grave.   Caithness flagstone clearly allowed attention
to detail of finish, particularly of dry-stone walling, but
field work clearly shows that, although the presence of
such fine building material in Caithness may have
modified the plan of certain cairns, it certainly did not
dictate them.

Fig. 13 illustrates the three basic plans.   The *Camster
type* is enclosed in a circular cairn, the *Yarrows type*
in a long cairn with prominent pairs of projecting
cairn material at each end (*horns*).   This is termed a
long-horned cairn.   The *Ormiegill type*, although lacking

the length of the Yarrows type, is also a horned cairn, a *short-horned cairn*. Excavation has not so far revealed any long-horned cairn in which a chamber was entered from each forecourt, although one short-horned cairn in Caithness had a chamber at each end. This was discovered during excavation, and preliminary field work had not given any indication of it.

In addition to the Camster, Yarrows and Ormiegill

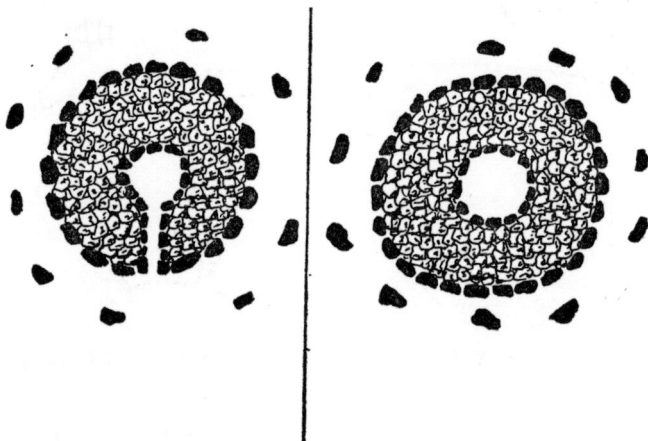

Fig. 14. Clava cairns; Passage grave and ring cairn.

types, there is a fourth group with a more restricted distribution around the northern end of the Great Glen. This is the *Clava group*, and consists of simple passage graves set in circular cairns and *ring cairns*. The latter are probably derived from the former, but in place of a central covered chamber approached by a roofed passage, there is an unroofed circular area at the centre of the cairn, but without any passage to the side of the cairn. In both types there is usually an outer free-standing stone circle set concentrically with the cairn.

(d) *The Orkneys.* It is obvious that developments on the Scottish mainland would have influenced those of the Orkneys, and this is apparent in field work. Cairns of both Camster and Yarrows type are known. In addition, a development of the Camster type may be seen, in which the chamber of the typical Camster

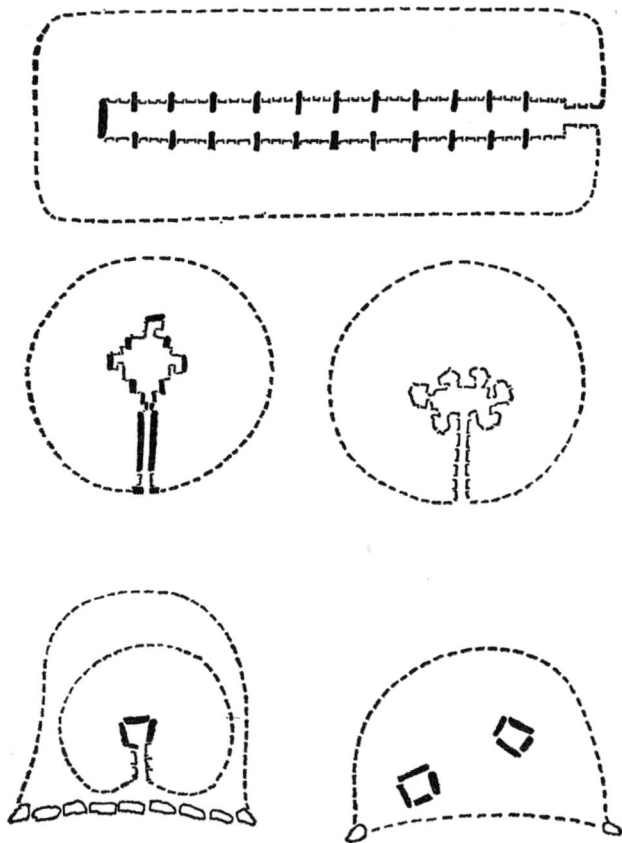

Fig. 15. *Upper:* stalled cairn. *Middle:* Maes Howe types. *Lower:* Heel-shaped cairns.

cairn becomes progressively elongated. In its extreme form it is known as a *stalled cairn*, in which there is a long chamber with side walls of dry-stone walling and which is segmented by pairs, sometimes as many as fourteen pairs, of opposed orthostats projecting into the chamber. Such chambers were normally enclosed in long cairns. The latter are not to be regarded as part of the long-cairn tradition which is known elsewhere in Britain, but are the result of the structural necessity of covering an abnormally elongated chamber (Fig. 15).

There is a third, and foreign, element represented by the *Maes Howe group*. Maes Howe is a magnificent *cruciform passage grave*, that is a passage grave with one end and two side chambers arranged, with the passage, in the form of a cross. This plan is distinctive of the Boyne Culture of Ireland (see below, page 64). It undergoes a development in Orkney in which the number of side chambers is increased until we reach the stage represented by *Holm of Papa Westray*, with its multitude of side chambers. As in the development of stalled cairns, so in this we can see the evolution of a long cairn purely as a structural necessity.

(e) *The Shetlands*. The most recent survey of chambered cairns in the Shetlands lists fifty-seven examples, but it is probable that more remain to be identified. The majority are *heel-shaped cairns*, so named from the plan of the enclosing cairn, which resembles the heel of a shoe. Chambers are in the passage-grave tradition, and may be either rectangular or cruciform in plan. There are also round and even square cairns containing chambers, also apparently in the passage-grave tradition. In addition, there are cairns of varying plan which appear to contain closed cists and which nevertheless appear to belong to the main Shetland tradition (Fig. 15).

THE CHAMBERED CAIRNS OF IRELAND

In discussing the chambered cairns of Ireland it is more convenient to discuss them on a typological, rather than on a geographical, basis. Four main types may be identified, wedge-shaped cairns, passage graves, horned and court cairns (taken together) and portal dolmens. There is, in addition, a small group of entrance graves in south-east Ireland, similar to those of the Scillies (see above, page 50), and the two groups are usually linked and referred to as the *Scilly–Tramore group*.

(a) *Wedge-shaped Cairns*. This is the most numerous and widely spread type of cairn in Ireland, although the greatest density lies in the south-west. It is a measure of the need for further field work that to date a comprehensive distribution map of these cairns has not been published. Such a study might reveal the existence of regional groups, such as has been suggested for the area north of the Sperrin Mountains in the north of the country.

Unlike the majority of long cairns so far discussed, with the exception of the Kent group (see above, page 56), the wedge-shaped cairn is the only one which may confidently be classified as a gallery grave. The chamber consists of a rectangular gallery built of orthostats, often decreasing in width and height towards the rear, and sometimes with a small closed chamber at the inner end. In many cairns there is also a small ante-chamber or *portico* at the entrance, which faces in a westerly direction, unlike the majority of long cairns so far discussed. The typical enclosing cairn is short in relation to its width, and often tapers inwards from front to rear, hence the name, *wedge-shaped cairn*. The rear end is sometimes flat, sometimes rounded. At the broad end there is sometimes a *flat frontal façade*, a line of orthostats. One or more inner walls, built of orthostats, may be identified in the body of the cairn between the chamber and the peristalith.

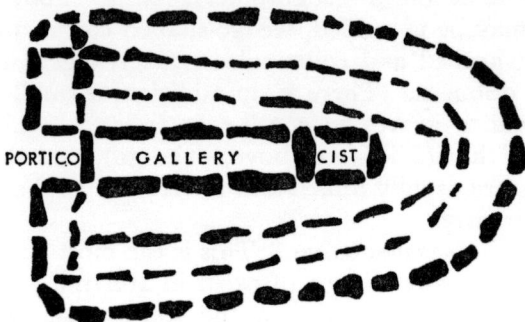

PORTICO   GALLERY   CIST

Fig. 16.

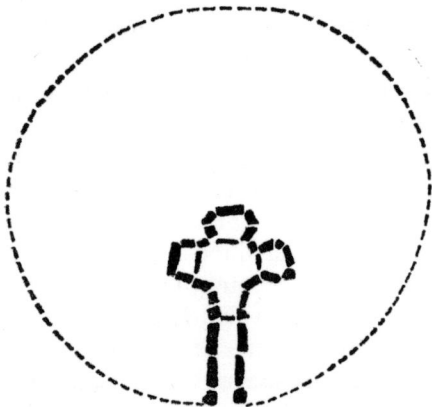

Fig. 17.

(b) *Passage Graves.* There are a few simple passage graves in Ireland, but a common form is the *cruciform passage grave*, in which two side chambers and one end chamber open from the main chamber and, with the passage, give the type its distinctively cross-shaped plan. In some cairns an additional pair of side chambers was occasionally added. The chamber proper often has a fine corbelled roof (Fig. 17).

Cairns of this type, together with associated small finds, are usually grouped together as the *Boyne Culture* so named from a small concentration of such cairns in the valley of the River Boyne. In addition to this passage-grave 'cemetery' there are three other main concentrations or cemeteries, Loughcrew in Co. Meath, Carrowkeel and Carrowmore, both in Co. Sligo. This grouping together of passage graves into cemeteries— at Loughcrew there are some thirty cairns within a small area—contrasts with the more scattered distribution of most other types of chambered cairn in the British Isles.

In several cairns roofing slabs and orthostats are decorated with various motives, including triangles, lozenges, spirals and zigzags. This *megalithic art*, as it is usually called, is discussed later in this chapter (see below, page 79).

(c) *Horned and Court Cairns*. We have already encountered horned cairns in Scotland, both those in the north, with their projecting 'horns', and those in the south-west, which have semicircular forecourts. More than 200 Irish horned cairns have been identified from field work, much of it recent, and they are found mostly north of a line drawn between Dundalk and Galway City. They resemble in a general way those of south-west Scotland in their trapezoidal cairns, usually with an orthostatic peristalith, in their crescentic or semi-circular orthostatic façades at the eastern and broader end, and in their segmented chambers. It has been suggested that the horned cairns of both countries should be grouped together under the heading of the

E

Clyde–Carlingford Culture, but because of differences of structural detail and associated finds it is preferable to treat the Irish cairns as a separate group and to refer to them and their associated small finds as the *Carling-*

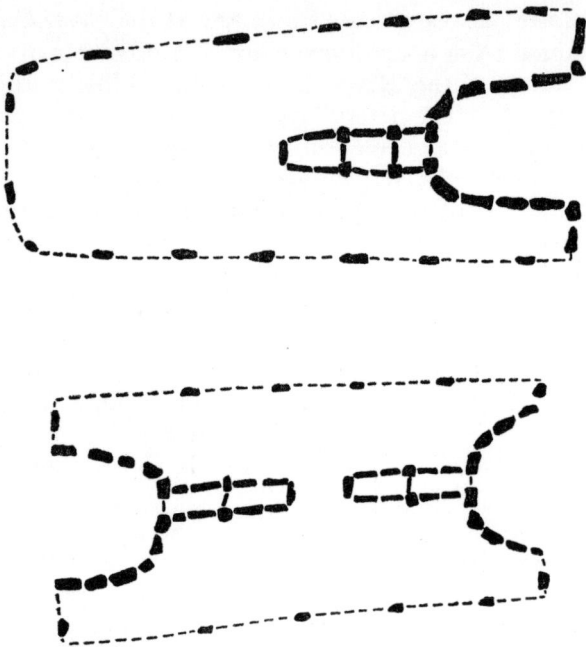

Fig. 18. *Upper:* Horned cairn. *Lower:* Double-horned cairn.

ford Culture—named after Carlingford Lough, around which there is an important cluster of cairns (Fig. 18).

It has recently been suggested that the term 'horned cairn' should be abandoned in place of 'court cairn', but as the former has been in use for many years and as the term is used on some Ordnance Survey maps, it seems preferable to retain it. The term *court cairn* may then be restricted to describe those cairns in which there is an enclosed open space or *court* leading into the chamber, in contrast with the open forecourt of the horned cairn. In some cairns there is a forecourt and segmented chamber at each end, the *double-horned cairn*.

Field work reveals that court cairns are concentrated

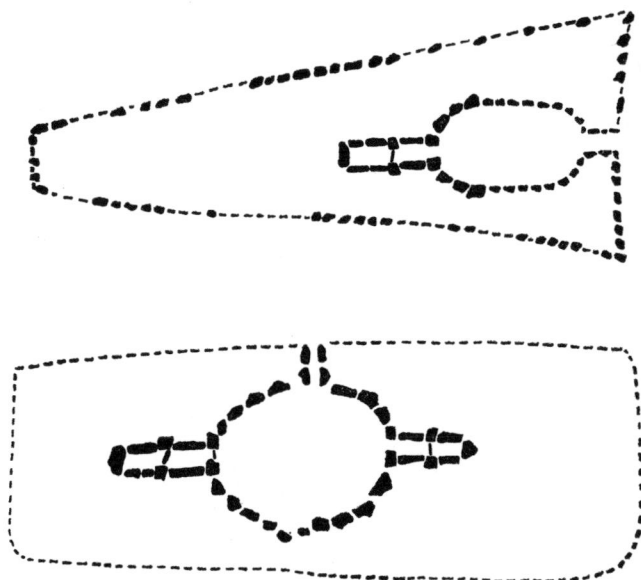

Fig. 19. Court cairns.

in the extreme west, and it seems probable that the type evolved in part from an increase in the size of the façade, so that it progressively produced a closed court, with a narrow access passage. Some court cairns have chambers opening from opposed sides of a central court. This is, in effect, a double-horned cairn in which a pair of chambers, each with its forecourt, was placed forecourt to forecourt, instead of the chambers being placed back to back. This may also have contributed to the original idea of the court cairn (Fig. 19).

(d) *Portal Dolmens*. The main features of the portal dolmen have already been described (see above, page 51), and the Irish examples, the majority of which lie in the east of the country, resemble those of western Britain. Irish portal dolmens are often considered to have been derived from horned cairns, but there are equally strong arguments to suggest the contrary.

The main types of chambered cairn in Britain and Ireland have been discussed at some length, as together they constitute one of the most important surviving types of monument in the stone-bearing regions of these islands. They also illustrate in their regional diversity of type the prime importance of field work, for it is primarily from field surveys that our present knowledge is derived. It is probable that several more remain to be recognised, as there are gaps in the known distribution which occur in areas which would appear to have been attractive to the Neolithic people who were mainly responsible for their construction. The cairns as a whole are to be found mainly in areas of small present-day population and, as recent discoveries in Scotland, Wales and Ireland have shown, structures such as these may pass unnoticed by the untutored eye. A well-informed local archaeologist has the best chance of discovering new sites, for it is his detailed local knowledge which will enable him to seek in the most promising areas and, with luck, to discover and to identify.

The plans which illustrate this section have been drawn as an aid to recognition. They have been chosen in an attempt to portray the commonest type of chambered cairn in each of the several areas defined. It must be remembered, however, that most are plans based on excavated sites and that the majority of cairns, particularly unexcavated cairns, will reveal only a proportion of the structural features shown here. The average site today will appear in the field as a stone-built mound of varying size, usually partially or completely grass-grown. There will be hollows in the mound, some caused by stone-robbing and others marking the position of disturbed chambers. The plan of the latter will not be always immediately comprehensible, as some orthostats may have been removed and others disturbed. In many instances a full appreciation of the structure is not possible until a plan has been drawn (Plate II *upper*).

Despite this, the study of chambered cairns in the field has much to offer the field archaeologist. Not only is there the possibility of the discovery of a hitherto unrecognised site but also many known sites have not been adequately planned or published, a lack which is felt by many students of chambered cairns.

BURIAL MOUNDS—UNCHAMBERED CAIRNS

Although many hundreds of unchambered cairns survive throughout the stone-bearing areas of Britain and Ireland, they do not offer in external diversity of plan the same variety as do chambered cairns. This does not mean that internal diversity of burial ritual, and sometimes of structure, did not exist, but any such diversity may be identified only by excavation. It must be remembered that it would be impossible to determine, too, whether a completely undisturbed round cairn was chambered or unchambered, unless there was visible evidence of an orthostat or a capstone. Even where the latter is visible, it might be impossible to determine whether this was the capstone of a burial chamber or merely the cover of a cist.

Unchambered cairns are circular in plan and vary in diameter from as little as 15 feet to as much as 200 feet, and in height from 1 or 2 feet to 20 feet or more (Fig. 20). It is not possible to attribute a cairn to any particular period on the basis of superficial appearance alone. Only excavation can accurately determine its cultural and chronological position. It must also be appreciated that not all stone mounds were necessarily

Fig. 20.

built to cover burials. Many groups of small cairns in upland counties are found clustered together near the edges of field systems, either ancient or modern, and it is possible that mounds in some of these clusters are *clearance cairns*—mounds accumulated by the throwing together of stones collected from fields. Some such clearance cairns are marked as burial mounds on some Ordnance Survey maps. Cairns have also been built in more recent times to commemorate events such as battles or the mustering of Highland regiments, but details of such mounds are normally known locally, and are unlikely to be confused with burial cairns. Cairns of more casual construction have also accumulated in mountainous areas as a result of passers-by each depositing a stone.

It is usually possible to distinguish a true burial

mound from other mounds. Burial cairns are normally well built and not haphazardly thrown together, as were clearance cairns and some other types of casual mound. Many unchambered cairns of the Bronze Age are prominently sited on the tops of hills or in other conspicuous positions (Plate II *lower*).

STONE CIRCLES, ALIGNMENTS AND OTHER STANDING STONES

In many areas of south-west and northern England, in Wales, Scotland and Ireland there are various settings of standing stones. The number of visible stones in any particular setting varies considerably, but two main categories may be distinguished, the stone circle and the alignment. Sometimes the two types are combined in the one structure.

STONE CIRCLES

An immediate distinction must be drawn between simple stone circles, in which the uprights are not associated with an enclosing bank and ditch, and henge-monuments.

(a) *Simple Stone Circles.* As the name implies, this is a setting of upright stones, circular in plan, which has no apparent practical use, other than that of delimiting a circular area. Some circles have at their centre one or more free-standing monoliths. It is immediately obvious on visiting a stone circle that such sites could never have formed part of a domestic or defensive structure. Although dating evidence is meagre, even from excavated sites, it is now generally accepted that they date from the Bronze Age and that their use was ritual. They are best regarded as ritual meeting-places, sometimes associated with internal burial mounds. The latter appear to date from the earlier part of the Bronze Age, but towards the end of the period the ritual aspect appears to have predominated over the funerary (Fig. 21).

Although there is some variation in both size of stones and diameter of circle, it is not yet possible to define regional groups. Diameters may vary from a few feet to more than 400 feet. Some large circles survive in the north of England. The majority of stone circles in Cornwall and Wales are quite small, mostly

Fig. 21.

between 60 and 80 feet in diameter. Those of Scotland are similar, as are those of Ireland, where they are widespread. The height of individual stones varies from a few feet to more than 10 feet.

Variations in size are possibly to be related in direct proportion to the size and resources of the community who built them. The variety of plan discernible among chambered cairns is in part a reflection of the different cultural groups who built and used them. In the same way the apparent homogeneity, other than size, of stone circles as a class possibly reflects the greater cultural unity of Britain and Ireland during the middle and later parts of the Bronze Age. Perhaps we should not assume, however, that more detailed study would not reveal some regional variation.

Some stone circles are concentric with a low inner burial cairn. A localised variant of this, probably dating to the Early Bronze Age, is represented by a group of more than seventy *recumbent stone circles* found in north-east Scotland in the counties of Aberdeen, Kincardine and Banff. The uprights of these circles decrease in height from two tall stones (*flankers*) which stand on each side of a prostrate monolith (the

Fig. 22.

recumbent)—the latter sometimes measuring as much as 16 feet long and 8 feet high, and having a flat upper surface. Small recumbent stone circles are also known in Ireland, notably in Co. Cork. They differ from the Scottish, both in that the two tallest stones of the circle are set diametrically opposite to the recumbent and in the absence of a central burial cairn (Fig. 22).

(b) *Henge Monuments*. The *henge monument* is a ritual structure in which a circular setting of monoliths, wooden posts or pits was enclosed by a bank and ditch. The ditch, merely a quarry ditch, normally lies immediately inside the bank, although at Stonehenge the ditch is outside the bank. The name *henge* or henge monument is, of course, derived from Stonehenge, the *henge* element coming from an Anglo-Saxon word implying 'hanging', and referring to the horizontal lintels of the structure.

Stonehenge itself has a complex arrangement of upright stones, which date from two major structural phases during the Early Bronze Age, and which are enclosed within a circular earthwork of Neolithic date. Avebury is also a henge monument, consisting of two large stone circles surrounded by a third, very large

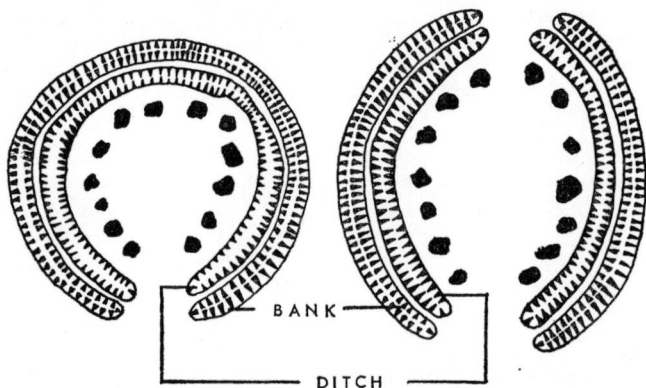

Fig. 23. Henge monuments. *Left:* Class I. *Right:* Class II.

stone circle set on the inner lip of a deep ditch, which has a massive external bank. It will be appreciated that these two sites are exceptional in their complexity of plan. A single circular setting of monoliths set concentrically within a bank and ditch is usual in stone-built henge monuments.

Henge monuments as a class, whether the internal structure was stone or wood built, or was simply an arrangement of pits, may be subdivided into those with single entrances (class I) and those with diametrically opposed twin entrances (class II). Class I structures appear to date from the Neolithic period and class II from the transitional period between the Neolithic and the Early Bronze Age. Henge monuments have been identified in Britain from Dorset to Orkney and from Cornwall to Norfolk (Fig. 23). They are also known in Ireland.

Like the simple stone circles of the Bronze Age, they appear to have been built for ritual purposes, sometimes perhaps, as also in the case of simple stone circles, involving the observation of the sun, moon or stars. Some early henge monuments were burial places in which cremations were placed in a circular setting of pits within a banked enclosure. Stonehenge in its first phase was one such site, known as a *cremation cemetery* (see below, page 131), and the stone structures as we know them today were added later. In the later henge monuments the purely ritual, as opposed to the burial, element appears to have predominated. Although burial within the banked enclosure was no longer practised, later peoples often chose to build their burial mounds close to henge monuments.

ALIGNMENTS

An *alignment* or *stone row* is, as the name suggests, a linear setting of monoliths. There are usually one or two parallel rows, sometimes three, as on Dartmoor, and up to as many as twenty-two rows in Caithness. Alignments may vary in length to a maximum of more than one mile, but neither the original length nor the total number of monoliths originally erected can be determined without excavation. In many surviving alignments, for example, there are gaps in the usually even spacing, suggestive of missing or fallen and buried stones. Surviving stones vary in height above ground from a few inches to more than 20 feet, but in some areas stones may be buried partially in peat.

Alignments may be associated with simple stone circles and burial cairns, but without excavation it cannot be assumed that each part of a composite structure was built at the same time.

As with simple stone circles, there has been little recent detailed study of alignments, and it is difficult even after excavation to date such sites accurately. More detailed field work would undoubtedly add to our knowledge of these sites, but even a cursory survey reveals local variants. There are some sixty alignments on Dartmoor, consisting of one, two or three parallel rows of stones. The average length of the alignment is between 400 and 500 feet, although longer settings are known. Individual stones rarely exceed 3 feet in height, although, again, there are exceptions. It has been noted that many are aligned with an east–west orientation.

At the opposite end of Britain some dozen alignments have been recorded in Caithness. Here, as in Devon, individual stones are small, but examples of six, thirteen, twenty and twenty-two rows are known in the county. Some of these settings are structurally associated with small cairns. Elsewhere in Britain there are about eight small alignments in Wales, and the remains of a few in the north of England, east of the Pennines. The latter, such as the three surviving *Devil's Arrows* near Boroughbridge in Yorkshire, may be the remains of larger alignments and the height of the surviving monoliths, one of which stands more than 20 feet above the present ground surface, suggests that these sites were once very much more visually impressive than those of either Dartmoor or Caithness.

There are fewer known alignments in Ireland, although there are several in Counties Tyrone and Fermanagh, north of the Sperrin Mountains, where they are sometimes structurally associated with stone circles. Elsewhere in the country alignments are thinly but widely spread.

OTHER STANDING STONES

Settings of monoliths, whether linear or circular in plan, offer many problems of interpretation, which even excavation is frequently unable to clarify. It is probably for this reason that they have not been studied systematically in recent years. As we have seen, it is not possible without excavation to know how many monoliths originally stood in either an alignment or a stone circle. In the same way a single standing stone or *menhir* (in Irish *gallán*, *dallán* or *liagán*) was erected to stand independently or originally formed part of a setting of stones.

Single standing stones were erected to serve a variety of purposes, and their use extended in time at least from the Bronze Age to the early medieval period. The tradition of ritual use of single standing stones continued after the introduction of Christianity into Britain and Ireland, both in the erection of stone crosses and in their adaptation for Christian use by inscribing a cross on a prehistoric standing stone. Burials of Bronze Age date have been found at the base of menhirs, but it cannot always be shown that the erection of the menhir and the burials were contemporary, although this is frequently probable. In the Iron Age standing stones in Ireland were sometimes carved with Celtic decorative motives, presumably for ritual purposes. Standing stones were also used in the same period, possibly in various ritual and ceremonial gatherings, at important sites such as Tara. It is also possible that single stones may have marked boundaries and roadways.

A problem of interpretation common to the study of stone circles, alignments and menhirs is that a setting of monoliths or a single monolith may today represent the sole visible remains of a hitherto more complex monument. A stone circle, for example, may represent the remains of the perimeter of a burial cairn from which all other traces have been removed. It is sometimes possible to recognise such a structure, as in many cases the upright stones may be smaller and flatter than those of a free-standing stone circle, and they may be closely set, sometimes almost contiguous. Remains of the peristalith of a cairn may be smaller in diameter than other stone circles in the neighbourhood. In a few instances the stones may lean uniformly outwards, caused by the pressure of the now vanished cairn. A circular setting of upright stones may also represent part of the foundations of a circular hut, or even a badly ruined stone fort, but close attention to other surface features in the vicinity will generally allow the correct interpretation to be made.

Single standing stones have often been erected in recent times as scratching posts for cattle. They may be sometimes recognised by their isolated position in the centre of a field. Occasionally local tradition and place-names may help in determining whether or not a standing stone is of recent erection. Pairs of standing stones may sometimes be found in central Scotland, where one of the pair is often pillar-like and the other more triangular in shape. A closely set pair of stones may originally have formed the entrance jambs into a now destroyed hut, fort or other enclosure.

The correct interpretation in the field of standing stones requires a little experience, but as we have seen, a final decision cannot be made in many cases until after excavation. Systematic field work would undoubtedly contribute to a greater understanding of stone circles, alignments and menhirs, not only by the correct identification of hitherto unrecognised sites but also in the production of adequate plans and the probable elimination from consideration of sites which are of recent date.   This is a task which might well be undertaken by young archaeologists who live in areas where sites of these types are known, or whose existence is possible on grounds of geology and general distribution.

DECORATED AND INSCRIBED STONES

Reference has been made in this chapter to decorated and inscribed stones.   Decoration may take the form of various motives carved on flat wall or roof surfaces

Fig. 24.

of chambered cairns and cists and on rock surfaces. Standing stones also carry a variety of motives, funerary and ritual, both pre-Christian and Christian.

Megalithic Art.   Decoration on roofing stones and orthostats of chambered cairns (hence the name, *megalithic art*) is restricted almost entirely to sites of the Boyne Culture in Ireland and Anglesey (see above, page 64).   Motives carved or pecked on the flat face of structural stones include lozenges and triangular patterns, series of concentric circles and spirals, wheel-like and zigzag motives. Most of this has the appearance of abstract art, but some of these patterns are occasionally used together to produce an eye-like or a face-like motive. More rarely, some of the motives are so arranged as to portray in a very stylised manner the human figure, possibly a representation of some sort of female deity (Fig. 24).

Cup-and-ring Markings. This motive, which consists of a central hollow depression (*cup*) surrounded by one or more circular or penannular grooves (*rings*), is known in many parts of upland Britain and Ireland. The cup motive, several occurring on the same surface, without rings, is found in greater numbers in the same areas. Cup-and-ring markings have been found on cover slabs of stone cists, on boulders and rock outcrops. As cup-and-ring markings are sometimes known in areas where there are known to have been deposits of copper in prehistoric times, as in south-west Ireland, Wales and Scotland, it has been suggested that these motives were in some way connected with metal prospecting. Were this so, it would appear that the designs had some ritual, rather than metallurgical, significance, but recognition of the possibility of such an association may contribute to the location of hitherto unknown markings.

Standing Stones. Cup-marks have also been recognised on standing stones forming part of stone circles. In addition, other carvings are known, which range widely in date and which were not necessarily contemporary with the erection of the stones on which they were carved.

It was only as recently as 1953 that carvings of axe-heads and a dagger were recognised at Stonehenge. Their almost complete obliteration and the fact that they had not been recognised previously on what must be one of the most thoroughly examined prehistoric sites in Europe, makes it all the more important that all standing stones should be examined carefully for similar evidence. In this, no attempts should be made to scrape away moss or any other vegetable cover on the surface of the stone. The carvings at Stonehenge were first recognised in favourable lighting conditions, and a field archaeologist anxious to examine other structures for similar evidence should visit such sites on different occasions in varying lighting conditions. Bright sunlight is not always suitable for this.

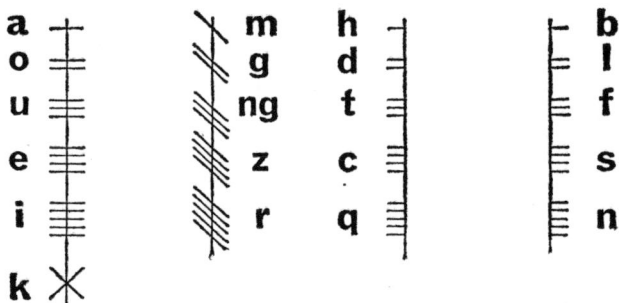

Fig. 25.

Ogam Stones. The *Ogam script* resembles a kind of visual Morse code, in which the letters of the Celtic alphabet are represented by short straight lines inscribed on standing stones. Each letter is represented by lines up to five in number and so arranged, either that they cross a central vertical line at right angles or diagonally, or that they are set to one side only, and at right angles to the central line. The vertical line is often the straight edge of the standing stone (Fig. 25).

The ogam inscription normally commemorates an individual and gives his name and his descent, such as

F

SAGRANI, SON OF CUNOTAMUS. A small proportion of stones have bilingual inscriptions, the same legend being inscribed in both provincial Latin and ogam. Some stones also include the words, HIC IACIT—'here lies (the body of) . . .', showing that they are simple grave stones.

The majority of ogam stones are to be found in Ireland, particularly in the south-west, in Counties Kerry and Cork and in Co. Waterford, but they are also found as far north as Co. Antrim and elsewhere in the country. In Britain they are found in areas which received either immigrants or influences from Ireland in the late Roman period and following centuries. These include Wales, Cornwall and western Scotland. They are also found elsewhere in Scotland from Shetland to Perthshire.

Other Stones with Early Christian Inscriptions and Symbols. In addition to ogam stones there are also numbers of stones inscribed with inscriptions and other symbols dating to the early centuries of Christianity in these islands. These include flat grave slabs in Ireland with a simple inscription such as OR DO AIGIDIU, an abbreviation of 'Oroit do Aigidiu', literally, 'a prayer for Aigidiu', or as we might say, 'pray for the soul of Aigidiu'. In this instance the inscription lies alongside an incised ornamental cross. Simple and ornamental crosses and simple representations of the Crucifixion are frequently found without an accompanying inscription. Similarly, grave slabs are sometimes found with a name only inscribed on it, as CORCRAIN, modern 'Corcoran'. Many inscribed stones of this type in Ireland are found on or near the sites of Early Christian monasteries (see below, page 132). They contributed in part to the development of the great series of Irish high crosses and scripture crosses of later centuries.

Pictish Symbol Stones. At about the same time as

these developments were taking place in Ireland, north-east Scotland also witnessed the development of a tradition of stone-carving. This evolved its own highly distinctive repertoire of motives from a variety of different sources. The designs include various abstract motives, such as the crescent and V-rod, the double-disc

Fig. 26.

and Z-rod, a mirror-like pattern and several others (Fig. 26). Various animals are also represented, including fish, birds, bull, boar, wolf or dog, stag and horse and a fabulous elephant-like creature. The earlier designs were incised on roughly dressed slabs or on boulders, and the later were carved in relief on large upright slabs. The latter also occasionally include probable Christian motives, such as the cross, often combined with elaborate interlacing patterns.

It is probable that these symbol stones were erected to serve some ritual or religious purpose, but the exact meaning of the symbolism eludes us today. They were carved by the people who emerge in history as the Picts, and are found in the Pictish area to the north of the Forth, with a few in north-west and south-west Scotland.

Decorative stones have been found incorporated as building material or used as gate-posts in structures dating to periods subsequent to the original use of such stones. The field archaeologist should be aware of this and examine in appropriate areas buildings which might incorporate decorated stones.

CHAPTER V

Field Monuments

FORTIFIED SITES

STONE-BUILT fortified sites of prehistoric or early historic date survive in very large numbers in both Britain and Ireland. In their present ruined and grass-covered condition it is not always possible, without excavation, to determine whether a fortified site was stone-built, constructed from earth and timber or was built from a combination of both techniques. This is particularly true of hill-forts in certain parts of Britain. A study of local solid geology, however, may allow one to determine which type of construction was likely to have been used in a fort, where this is not immediately apparent from surface indications. We shall first examine hill-forts, followed by other native fortified sites, Roman forts and other military works.

HILL-FORTS

In this section we are primarily concerned with the hill-forts of upland Britain. Earth and timber forts of the lowland areas are referred to in Chapter VII, although the earthen ramparts of some of these were sometimes reconstructed in prehistoric times by the addition of a stone facing.

Stone-built hill-forts are widespread in Wales, northern England, southern and central Scotland. In their present state the appearance of their defences varies from well-defined and massive stone walls, very occasionally preserving such details as a rampart walk, to low, scattered heaps of stone without visible evidence of inner or outer facing. Such walls were normally fronted by rock-cut ditches, from which some of the material for the construction of the walls was obtained. The defences were pierced by one or more entrances, at which the line of the wall was often inturned at each side to form a short passage. These entrances would originally have been closed by strong wooden doors, and it may be possible for the pivot stones, on which such doors would have turned, to be identified on some sites. Some forts were *multivallate*, having more than one line of defensive wall and ditch. In such forts the successive rings of fortifications were normally concentric and set in close proximity to each other, so as to give extra depth to defence.

The present appearance of stone ramparts rarely provides visible evidence of their internal structure. It may be assumed, however, that some forts were provided with an internal timber bracing. This may be proved by excavation, but in Scotland and Wales the so-called *vitrified fort* sometimes allows this conclusion to be drawn without excavation. Timbers in the thickness of the wall, and perhaps also lean-to structures at the inner face of the wall, were sometimes accidentally or intentionally set on fire by friend or enemy. The resultant blaze, often fanned by high winds, fused the stonework into solid vitrified, or glass-like masses. Quantities of vitrified stone may be easily recognised in the mass of standing or fallen wall material.

As the name suggests, hill-forts may be found in upland country, but absolute height above sea-level in itself was not important to their builders. Some hill-forts were built at a relatively low elevation, but even a low hill in level countryside sometimes gave the defenders of a hill-fort the necessary defence in an age when the range of missiles was limited to that of the arrow, the spear and the sling-stone. A gently rounded hill-top site was preferred, around which a ditch could be dug and ramparts erected, both following the contour of the hill. In some instances the slope of the hill was sufficiently steep to require the minimum of artificial defences around much of its perimeter. More vulnerable sectors were protected by stronger defences, particularly near entrances which, for convenience of access, could not be situated on precipitous slopes.

A very small proportion of hill-forts has been excavated, and it is therefore not yet possible to define regional groups in any detail, although it is becoming clear that such a definition should be possible. Some of the criteria necessary for any such differentiation must, of course, be based on the results of excavation. It is true, however, that a considerable contribution may be made by intensive local field survey and, indeed, for some time to come the results of systematic field work are likely to contribute as much to an over-all appreciation of hill-forts as the results of excavation. It must be remembered, too, that the study of stone-built forts cannot completely be divorced from that of other stone-built fortified sites of comparable date and of earth and timber hill-forts.

Hill-forts vary in area from defended sites enclosing as much as 100 acres or more to small sites covering less than 1 acre. The common factor is a perimeter defensive structure of wall and ditch, single or multiple. Variation in the total area enclosed by the defences was clearly governed by function. It is obvious that the smallest so-called hill-forts, which could never have contained more than a handful of huts, sometimes as few as three or four, are best interpreted as fortified settlements or defended homesteads. These small defended sites are evidence of the kind of response we should expect to have been made by a small community or single family group in an attempt to protect themselves and their possessions during a time of much unrest and uncertainty. They are not forts in the strict military sense, sites defended by armed soldiers, but merely amateur and personal—and perhaps successful—fortifications.

At the opposite extreme some of the largest hill-forts served as tribal capitals (sometimes referred to by their Latin equivalent of *oppida* (singular, *oppidum*)). Several tribal capitals have been identified in Britain, and sometimes the name of the tribe is known from Roman sources. It is possible that such capitals were permanently occupied by the tribal ruler and his court, together with other members of the tribe. The extent of the original occupation cannot always be determined without excavation, although traces of hut sites may be sometimes identified.

Coming between the tribal capitals and the fortified settlements or homesteads are medium-sized hill-forts. Some of these may have served as local points of tribal administration, as they are sometimes found in positions which suggest their domination of a well-defined geographical area. How far they were permanently occupied is difficult to determine without excavation, but it seems probable that many were occupied as refuges only in times of immediate external threat. Others may have held a small permanent population, but, on the whole, large permanent centres of population are rare in this context.

As far as we know, the various types of fortified sites

grouped together as hill-forts were built in the Celtic Iron Age, from approximately 300 B.C. until the arrival of the Romans in the first century A.D.   In areas outside effective Roman military control they continued in use beyond that date, and some were undoubtedly in use in post-Roman times.

Although so many factors concerning the interpretation of hill-forts may be appreciated only after excavation, the field archaeologist can contribute much by an intensive survey of a given area.   Only by such surveys can the number and proportion of sites of different acreages be known.   Remains of hut foundations may be identified in the interior.   Thorough survey may reveal details of the defences, particularly those of the entrances, and on very steep sites traces of collapsed walling may be identified lower down the hill.   This last may be of particular importance in showing that a hill-fort may have had more than one encircling wall. A detailed survey of a multivallate site may reveal evidence for a sequence of structural changes.

The *promontory fort* may be regarded as a variant of the true hill-fort.   In place of a continuous ring of defences, broken only by the entrances, advantage was taken of natural defences, particularly that of a projecting tongue of land with steep slopes on three sides.   It was necessary only to defend the fourth side, which otherwise would have been easy of access.   Defence was provided by a line, either univallate or multivallate, of bank and ditch.   Promontory forts are common in Cornwall, where they are sometimes known as *cliff castles*, in south Wales and in the south of Ireland. They may have either a coastal or an inland position.

As far as is known, most hill-forts were built before the arrival of the Romans in Britain.   This is true of the earth- and timber-built forts situated in areas which were under effective Roman control. In areas beyond such control, particularly in Wales and Scotland, hill-forts may have continued to be built, and certainly were in use, in post-Roman times. It is difficult without excavation, however, to identify such sites, still less to define any particular form of this type which may unequivocally be dated to the post-Roman period. It has been suggested that the so-called *nuclear fort* in Scotland is post-Roman in date, but this has not yet been proved to be so. It is a small circular or oval enclosure, rarely exceeding 100 feet in diameter and delimited by a thick stone wall. This citadel-like structure is often set at the centre of a hill-fort, the defences of which may already have been ruinous when the former was built, but which, even in their ruined state, would have given some added protection from attack.

OTHER NATIVE FORTIFIED SITES

In addition to hill-forts, whose defences followed the contours of hill-top sites, a number of other types of stone-built defensive structures were built in Scotland, particularly in the west and in the north, and in Ireland, where there are few hill-forts.

Scotland. One of the most impressive structures of this type is the *broch*, of which some 500 have been identified, having a markedly coastal distribution, mainly in the Western and the Northern Isles and the counties of Ross, Sutherland and Caithness. Although the broch may sometimes be built in a position of some natural strength, it does not normally rely on natural features for its defence. The broch is circular in plan, up to 60 feet or so in external diameter and with a wall thickness of up to 20 feet. A distinctive feature of its construction is the use of hollow walls, built either from ground level upwards or on a solid foundation. The inner face is normally vertical, but the outer face sometimes has an inward batter from near the base upwards, particularly in those brochs which were built to a height of 40 feet or more. It is obvious from the present appearance of many sites that few were built to this height, but it is equally obvious that broch dwellers relied primarily on the height of the walls for security. The outer face was unbroken apart from a small, low doorway, which could be securely barred from the inside (Plate III).

In several brochs it is possible to identify galleries within the wall structure. These were linked by flights of stone steps, of which many examples survive. These *intra-mural galleries*, as they are called, arose from the need to tie together the outer and inner shell of the broch as it rose from its foundations. They would also have served as convenient working platforms during construction, and later may have been used for storage. It is probable that there was originally a parapet walk. The taller brochs, in particular, would have served as admirable look-out posts.

Other internal features which may be recognised are small guard chambers built into the thickness of the wall on either side of the entrance, and one, or rarely, two *scarcements*. The latter is a narrow ledge or step on the inner wall-face which helped to support the roof of a lean-to timber structure built up against the inner wall of the broch, leaving a small open space at the centre. There was sometimes a well in this central area. Several brochs, particularly in Caithness and the Northern Isles, have traces of outworks, hut foundations and enclosures outside them. Whether or not these are contemporary with the use of the broch, their presence should be looked for in field survey.

Like the broch, the *dun* is a small dry-stone built defensive structure. It may be circular, oval, oblong or D-shaped in plan, often enclosing an area a little greater than that of a broch. The dun relied for defence in the thickness of its walls, which may measure up to 15 feet or more, but these were not built to a height comparable with that of some brochs. Broch-like features, however, may be identified, such as guard chambers and sometimes even a scarcement. Within the defended area there would probably have been a wooden hut or huts.

The *galleried dun*, as the name suggests, has galleries built into the thickness of the walls, but this is not to be confused with the true hollow-wall construction of the broch. Where stone stairs were built to give access to a parapet walk, they will normally be found built against the inner face of the dun and not in the thickness of the wall, as in the broch.

The word *dun* is Gaelic and means simply 'fort' or 'fortified place'. Its use in place-names does not necessarily imply that the site so-named is a dun of the type named here. It may be applied to a broch, a hill-fort or a castle, and even to natural features.

Associated perhaps with galleried duns is the *block house*, a fortified structure with internal gallery and some of the other structural features of a dun, but not enclosing an area. The few block houses so far identified in Scotland appear to be arc-shaped in plan and are sometimes built, as in the case of promontory forts, to defend a projecting tongue of land. Some block houses may have been free-standing, and others built into a stone wall of less elaborate construction, the whole complex in the latter case enclosing an area.

In the western coastal areas of the Scottish mainland and in the Western Isles there are many small forts, which have been referred to as *stack forts*. They differ from brochs and duns in that their construction appears to have been very much less elaborate and in their use of natural rocky features, particularly the steep-sided 'stack', which gives them their name.

The broch, the dun and the stack fort each appear to represent a local and specialised reaction in western and northern Scotland and in the Islands to the problem of defending a homestead or at most a very small settlement. As such, they may be considered as the counterpart of the small fortified homestead already referred to, and known from other parts of Britain, with which they appear to be broadly contemporary.

Ireland. One of the commonest surviving ancient sites in Ireland is the *ring fort*, normally a circular fortified area with defences built either of earth or of stone. In this book we may refer to the earthen ring fort as a *rath* (see below, page 126) and the stone-built ring fort as a *cashel* (from the Irish *caiseal*). Without excavation it is not always possible to determine whether a ring fort may be classified as a rath or cashel, and the difference between the two types is one of building materials, not one of function.

Cashels were sometimes built to take advantage of hill-top sites, but are more commonly found on level ground, although frequently in upland areas. They vary in size, but do not attain the extreme variations of the British hill-fort. The smaller, which may enclose an area only 50 feet in diameter, contained perhaps only one or two huts, and may be regarded as the Irish variant of the defended homestead. In keeping with their small size, their defences are similarly small in scale. The defences of the larger cashels, enclosing an

area as much as 200 feet in diameter, are correspondingly more massive and are forts in the strict sense of the
word.   Many of the larger sites measure up to 400 feet
in overall diameter, a considerable area being occupied
by double or triple walls.   The most common plan is
circular, but cashels of square, rectangular and D-
shaped plan are also known.

The walls of a cashel may be simple mounds of stone,
piled up in a manner similar to that of earthen banks.
More carefully built walls are also common, in which
an inner and outer face of well-chosen blocks enclose
an inner rubble core.   The larger forts sometimes have
chambers or galleries set in the thickness of the walls,
similar in purpose to those of the galleried duns of
Scotland (see above, page 92).   Inner stairways giving
access to parapet walks may survive in some forts,
notably in the south-west, and in such forts their truly
defensive character is emphasised by well-defended
entrances.   Many cashels have outer ditches, sometimes rock-cut, and in Co. Clare and the Aran Islands
chevaux de frise have been identified, settings of closely
set upright stones designed to impede attackers.

Cashels vary widely in date from the Bronze Age
until the Middle Ages, and this helps to explain the
very large number which survive.   There is ample
opportunity for detailed field studies of these sites in
Ireland, studies which should take note of overall and
inner dimensions, method of construction, position
and traces of internal structures.

ROMAN FORTS AND OTHER MILITARY WORKS

In contrast with native-built British and Irish
fortified sites, in which there is considerable variety of

plan and construction, Roman forts exhibit a uniformity of plan in keeping with their highly organised and disciplined military background. Stone-built Roman forts may conveniently be divided into two main classes, those built and maintained during the first three centuries of Roman rule, and those built in the last century of occupation. Each reflects the military situation of the time.

Under the first heading may be included the large legionary fortress, between 50 and 60 acres in extent, forts proper, normally between 2 and 10 acres in extent, and smaller fortified sites. Despite the variation in total area, the majority of fortresses and forts were built to a standard plan, normally rectangular with rounded corners, the proportion of length to breadth being approximately 3 : 2. It is common to compare such a plan with the shape of a playing card. Stone-built forts were often built to replace earlier earth and timber structures on the same site in periods when there was ample time for careful construction. The walls consisted of a concreted rubble core faced at front and rear by carefully squared blocks of uniform size. There was a gateway flanked by towers in each of the four sides. Internal towers were also built at each of the four corners and between each corner and gateway. An outer ditch was also normal. In the interior of such forts traces may survive of stone-built barrack blocks, stables, administrative buildings, granaries and workshops. A bath house was often built in a walled annexe outside the fort. The smaller fortlets are also normally rectangular in plan, but they may be square, and often have only one entrance.

Whereas stone-built forts of the first three centuries of Roman rule are widespread in Wales and the north of England, sites of the fourth century A.D. are to be found in coastal areas, particularly along the *Saxon Shore*, from the Wash to the Solent, but also in Wales. These later forts are more clearly defensive, as opposed to offensive, sites, and reflect in their design the last uneasy century of Roman rule when the Province was under seaborne attack from east and west. There is no uniformity of plan, but each Saxon Shore fort is distinguished by tall, thick walls and projecting bastions at the gateways and at intervals along the perimeter.

It is improbable that any stone-built Roman fortresses and forts remain to be discovered in Britain, but the field archaeologist should not, for this reason, neglect any opportunity to visit and study the known sites. Knowledge of the size and proportions of such structures may assist in the recognition of earth and timber forts which may yet be identified (see below, page 129).

Perhaps the most famous series of Roman remains in Britain is the complex of military works running from the Tyne to the Solway and known collectively as *Hadrian's Wall*. The wall proper is a stone structure surviving in various states of preservation along its length. Its construction is similar to that of the walls of forts, an inner concreted rubble core faced front and rear by blocks of regular size. Fronting the wall to the north along most of its length is a deep ditch, absent only where the wall is built close to the edge of an escarpment, and V-shaped in section. To the south is an earthwork, the *vallum*, a flat-bottomed ditch with low parallel banks set some distance away from both lips of the latter.

At varying intervals forts of varying size, but of standard plan, were built into the wall proper. At every Roman mile (approximately 1,620 yards), and built into the wall, there was a *milecastle*, a fortlet containing perhaps two small barrack blocks and two gate-

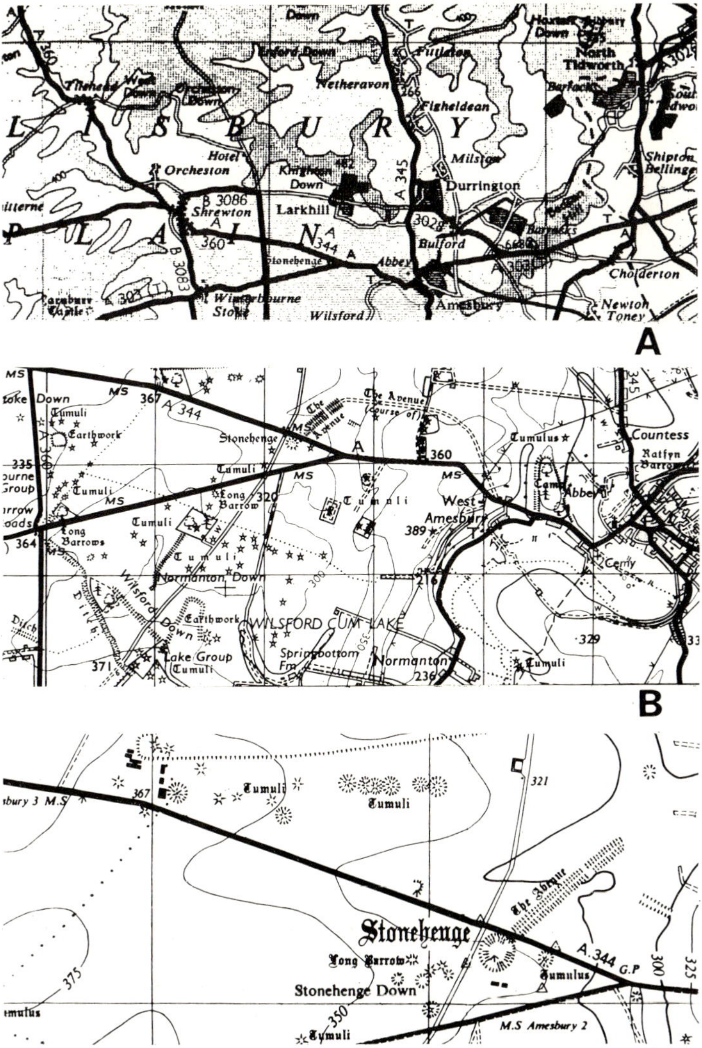

PLATE I. Position of Stonehenge as shown on A $\frac{1}{4}$-inch, B 1-inch and C $2\frac{1}{2}$-inch Ordnance Survey maps. (*Crown copyright reserved*)

PLATE II. *upper* Typical chambered cairn before excavation.

PLATE II. *lower* Typical round cairn before excavation.

ways allowing access through the wall. Between each pair of milecastles, and also built into the wall, were two *turrets*, small square structures with access only from the south. The whole complex of wall, forts, milecastles and turrets was connected by a rampart walk to allow continuous patrol. A military road for ease of communication was built between the wall proper and the vallum. Beyond the western limit of Hadrian's Wall at Bowness on Solway, the Cumberland coast was guarded by a series of milecastles and turrets, similar in plan and construction to those on the wall, but without the linking wall.

G

CHAPTER VI

Field Monuments

HABITATION SITES

WE have already seen that traces of huts and other structures may be recognised in the interior of fortified sites. We may now examine the evidence for stone-built habitation sites, prehistoric, Romano-British and post-Roman. The chapter concludes with some discussion of miscellaneous stone structures, including souterrains, temples and Early Christian religious sites.

PREHISTORIC HABITATION SITES

In contrast with ritual and fortified stone-built sites, the average domestic structure of prehistoric date

Fig. 27.

survives, if at all, merely as a foundation course. The most common structure of this type is the so-called *hut circle*, a ring of stones of varying size and perhaps incorporating small orthostats, which originally formed the foundations of a circular hut (Fig. 27). The upper part may have been built of timber, turf or sods, and roofed either by thatch or turf. Hut circles may date from Neolithic times, and circular huts continued in use throughout the Bronze and Iron Ages, the Roman period and into the Middle Ages. Without excavation it is not normally possible to date isolated hut circles, but some indication of their approximate date may occasionally be given by their association with other structures. Hut circles identified in the interior of a hill-fort may, for example, be contemporary with it, and therefore possibly of Iron Age date. The possibility must also be allowed, however, that huts might have been built some time after the construction of the fort.

There is some evidence to suggest that the climate may have been both drier and warmer during the Bronze Age than it is today. It would therefore have been possible for Man to have lived without too much discomfort in upland areas which have remained unoccupied since the end of the Bronze Age until today. It follows that many of these upland areas may have preserved remains of settlements. Some such areas have been studied, notably Dartmoor, where hut circles are often set in roughly circular enclosures known locally as pounds. A typical *pound*, which was probably a cattle enclosure, measures approximately 100 feet in diameter and its walls were stone-built. The foundation of the huts, too, are stone built, sometimes with an earthen bank heaped against the outer face. Similar hut circles are known on Bodmin Moor and in the moorland areas of Wales, northern England and in Scotland, even at altitudes as high as 1,500 feet. Some of these may also date from the Bronze Age. In some of these areas hut circles may partially be covered by peat which may have formed since the Bronze Age. It is common to find enclosures, bounded by roughly built dry-stone walling, associated with hut circles and which are probably remains of ancient *field boundaries* (see below, page 142). Clearance cairns may also be identified near hut circles and their associated field systems (see above, page 70).

Circular huts were also built in the Iron Age and, in southern Britain, during the Romano-British period. As we have seen, without excavation it is rarely possible to distinguish with any certainty huts of this period from other periods. Their position within a hill-fort, their association with a souterrain (see below, page 108) and the chance surface discovery of Iron Age or Romano-British pottery may nevertheless offer some suggestion of Iron Age or Romano-British date. In Scotland some well-built hut circles, approximately 30 feet in diameter, in which an outer and inner face enclosed a rubble core, have been shown by excavation to date from the Iron Age.

It is possible that the origins of the Irish clochán may date from the prehistoric period, although their use continued into the Middle Ages. A *clochán*, sometimes called a *bee-hive hut*, is a corbelled structure (for corbelling see above, page 46) in which the walls and roof are of dry-stone construction, the upper parts of the thick walls gradually coming inwards and merging with the corbelled roof. Some clocháns are circular in plan and may represent the earliest type. In this they resemble the circular chambers of some passage graves (see above, page 48), and this tradition of building may have survived from the Neolithic period. Later clocháns are of square or rectangular plan, and from medieval times onwards mortar was used to give extra stability to the structure.

In western and northern Scotland, and more particularly in the Isles, remains survive of a more
specialised form of circular stone-built hut, the *wheel-
house*. In this structure, usually measuring from
between 20 and 35 feet in diameter, short stone walls
were set radially to the outer circular wall, dividing
the outer area into a number of segments. The radial
walls do not extend into the central area, which
measures approximately 10 feet in diameter. Access
is sometimes possible from one segment to another

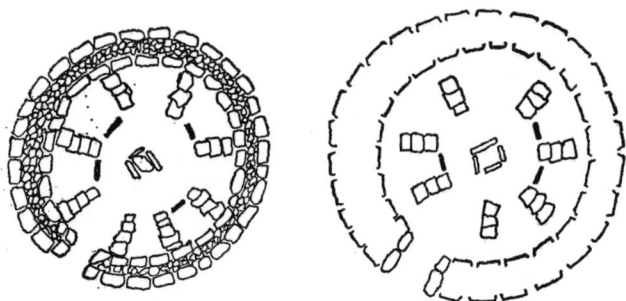

Fig. 28. *Left:* Wheel-house. *Right:* Aisled wheel-house.

through openings left in some of the radial walls (Fig.
28). A variant is the *aisled wheel-house*, in which the
outer ends of the radial walls did not extend as far as the
outer wall, a narrow gap being left between them. It
may be assumed that the radial walls were built as
supports for the roof, which may have been of slabs or
corbelling, or of timber and turf or thatch. The central
area, in which there was usually a hearth, may have
been left at least partially unroofed, to allow ventil-
ation. The wheel-house may be a stone-built version
of a timber hut and its origins date from the Iron Age.
It continued in use into the first two or three centuries
A.D. Remains of wheel-houses may sometimes be

identified within the ruins of a disused or dismantled broch.

It may be seen, therefore, that the majority of known remains of prehistoric hut foundations are circular in plan. Structures of differing plans were also built from the Neolithic period onwards. A few excavated huts of Neolithic date in both Britain and Ireland were rectangular, but this plan is not positively attested for either the Bronze or Iron Ages. The well-known coastal settlement of Skara Brae and the similar one at Rinyo in the Orkneys are unique, both in the plan of their huts, their internal furnishings and the fact that several huts were built close together, forming small hamlets in contrast with the individual homesteads known elsewhere at this period. The walls of the huts are dry-stone built, square in plan, with rounded corners and measure between 15 and 20 feet across. Stone-built fitted furniture, beds and dresser, fireplaces and cupboards built into the walls have survived. The properties of local flagstone, used so successfully in the contemporary chambered cairns of Caithness and Orkney, were appreciated. It is not impossible that similar sites may yet be identified in this area. Skara Brae was discovered after a violent storm which removed some of the sand which had hidden and preserved the settlement for many centuries.

A number of huts with stone foundations, belonging to a people with a Neolithic economy, although perhaps later in date than Skara Brae, have been recognised in Shetland, apparently associated with enclosures and field systems. The huts are usually roughly oval in plan and measure up to 50 feet in external length. Wall foundations are normally quite broad, up to 10 feet in thickness, and consist of an inner and outer face with a rubble core. Some houses have small recesses,

built into the thickness of the walls, and inner rooms.
They were approached through a narrow entrance
passage.   In the larger central area there was usually a
hearth.   It is possible that more sites of this type also
remain to be discovered, not only in the Northern Isles
but also on the mainland of northern Scotland.

This type of hut appears to have continued in use
during the local Bronze Age in Shetland, and has
features in common with the Iron Age courtyard house

Fig. 29.

of western Cornwall.   The *courtyard house* has an oval
plan and may measure as much as 90 feet in external
length.   A central courtyard is approached by a
narrow passage.   An end chamber, possibly serving as
the principal living-quarters for the family, and one or
more subsidiary side chambers—probably workshops
and store-rooms—open from the courtyard (Fig. 29).
Another structure, possibly of Iron Age date and
apparently confined to Caithness, is the *wag*.   This is
stone built, oval in plan and partially sunk into the
ground.   It is normally associated with a hut circle and
measures about twice the diameter of the latter.   The
wag proper is segmented by orthostats into compart-
ments which have been cattle stalls.

The present-day unexcavated appearance of the
different types of stone-built hut foundations varies

considerably. Often a hut circle will appear as a grass-grown ring-bank in which both stones and an entrance may be visible. Other sites will show as a scatter of stones over a circular area, and at first sight might be difficult to distinguish from a ruined cairn. In some instances it is not possible to positively classify such remains, although environment and geographical relationship to known structures may provide useful clues.

ROMANO-BRITISH HABITATION SITES

Even in areas of Britain which were fully and permanently under Roman control a considerable proportion of the population continued to live in settlement sites which had become traditional types during the preceding Iron Age. They may have acquired Roman pottery and trinkets, but it is not normally possible to know this without excavation. For this reason, when we speak of Iron Age huts in northern or south-west England or in Wales, we must also include those built and occupied in Roman and later times.

Certain elements of the native Celtic population, however, were encouraged to adopt a more Roman way of life, and this was partially achieved by the construction of town and country houses of a sophistication hitherto unknown in Britain. Some of these houses were probably built largely of stone, and others were half-timbered. The majority of the latter had stone foundations and were provided with tiled roofs, and it is therefore sometimes possible to identify their remains in field work.

The term *villa* is commonly used to denote a Romano-British country house, but there is much variety in ground plan which reflects both the degree of Roman-isation achieved and the wealth of the occupants. Essentially, the villa was the centre of a farm—using the term in its broadest sense—and the latter might have varied from a small agricultural unit, comparable in size with an average farm of today, to a large country estate. Excavation has shown that on certain sites

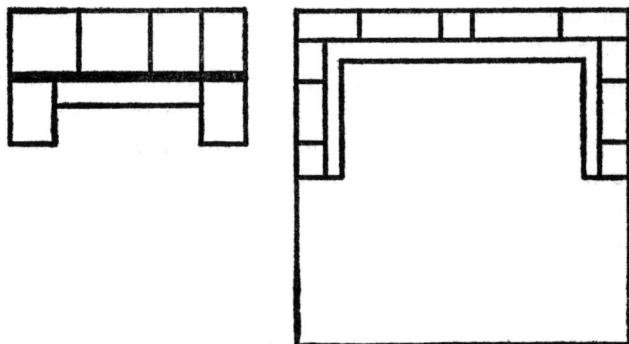

Fig. 30. Roman villas. *Left:* Winged corridor type. *Right:* Courtyard villa.

some degree of continuity may be traced from the small circular huts of pre- and early Roman times through a series of rebuilt and enlarged villas, which sometimes remained in occupation until the closing years of the Roman period.

The simplest type of villa is a rectangular building divided into four or five rooms, with a veranda running the whole length of the structure. The veranda was frequently replaced by a corridor built as an integral part of the villa and which connected the individual rooms. From this developed the *winged corridor type*, in which the end rooms projected forward of the front of the villa. A further development saw the extension of the 'wings', the outer ends of which were linked by either a wall or a fourth range of rooms to form the *courtyard villa*. The more elaborate villas sometimes consisted of two conjoined courtyard villas, the inner perhaps containing the private garden of the owner, and the outer serving as the farmyard.

Houses in Romano-British towns had varied plans and ranged from simple, long rectangular buildings, with one of the narrow ends fronting a street, to more elaborately planned dwellings, similar to the courtyard villa. The private house, of course, is only one type of structure the remains of which may be traced within the boundary of Romano-British towns. In addition, one would expect to find remains of other private and public buildings, such as inns, shops, public baths and temples. As it is improbable that hitherto unrecognised Romano-British towns are likely to be discovered, further reference is not made to them in this book.

The positive identification of hitherto unrecognised Romano-British villas may at first glance appear difficult, as the plan of a complex building of several rooms might be confused with the remains of a post-Roman structure. Grass-covered remains of stone-built foundations by themselves do not normally offer any accurate indication of date. There may be other evidence which might allow a more positive identification. Remains of a large medieval or later building will often be associated with documentary evidence, particularly if belonging to a monastic settlement. Reference to such sources as the Ordnance Survey's *Map of Monastic Britain* (see above, page 33) might be of assistance.

It is more probable that sites of Romano-British villas still awaiting discovery will be recognised not so much by visible traces of foundations as by other surface indications. In areas which have been extensively ploughed for many centuries visible traces of foundations will have disappeared, although the lowest courses may have survived underground. During ploughing, and more particularly deep ploughing, buried evidence may be brought to the surface and scattered over a field. This evidence may consist of broken pottery and glass, pieces of metal and broken bones. There may also be fragments of roofing tiles, small pieces of stone, brick and other building material. A scatter of pottery dating from any period may be of considerable assistance in locating buried structures. Similarly, the appearance of small fragments of stone concentrated in an area which otherwise is not stony may lead to the discovery of buried foundations and, if possible, aerial photographs of the area should be examined (see above, page 35).

POST-ROMAN HABITATION SITES

In the present state of knowledge little can be said about the stone-built or partially stone-built houses dating from the five centuries following the end of Roman Britain. The need here, as in so many other contexts, is for a planned programme of excavation on carefully chosen sites. Until this has been accomplished it will be possible only to offer generalisations about the kind of evidence which might emerge.

Although it is customary to speak of Roman and post-Roman Britain, it is generally difficult to draw a distinction between the two periods in terms of stone-built habitation sites in western and northern areas which had been under Roman control. It is becoming apparent from excavation that huts and houses, very similar to those of the Iron Age and Roman period, continued in use beyond the fifth century A.D. This is understandable, for in the west and north and in Ireland there was no great displacement of population. Pottery styles might change, as might foreign imports, but to simple peasant farmer and Celtic chieftain alike the collapse of the Roman Empire was hardly import-ant enough to cause him to alter his building traditions. This again means that only chance discovery of relevant surface finds is likely to be of significance in any attempt to date such structures.

MISCELLANEOUS STONE-BUILT STRUCTURES

(a) *Souterrains.* These as a class offer one of the most difficult problems of interpretation in British and Irish archaeology. They are found in Cornwall, Scotland and Ireland. Briefly, a *souterrain* is an underground structure in which a trench was cut in the subsoil, normally lined with dry-stone walling and roofed by stone slabs or, occasionally, by timber. Such a definition, however, conceals a considerable variety of plan which is best examined in relation to geo-graphical distribution.

Cornish souterrains, or *fogous* as they are known locally, are either slightly curved, sinuous or angled in plan, and measure 40 feet or more in length. They are usually about 5 feet wide and are sunk to a depth of about 6 feet into the subsoil. Walls are dry-stone built, normally with an inward batter, and the whole struc-ture roofed by flat slabs set on the walls. Earth and stone from the sloping trench, in which the souterrain was built, were usually piled on the roof. Some have small corbelled subsidiary chambers and more than one entrance. Cornish souterrains have been found

in association with courtyard houses (see above, page
103) and fortified sites, probably Iron Age or Romano-
British in date.

Scottish *earth houses*, as souterrains are generally called
in that country, are widely spread over much of the
eastern and northern mainland and in the Western and
Northern Isles. It is probable that detailed field work
would distinguish localised types, as have been recognised in Angus and parts of Perthshire. Some of the
latter, although exceptional, exceed 120 feet in length
and 8 feet in width, and have corbelled side chambers.
As in Cornwall, some other Scottish souterrains have
side chambers and more than one entrance. Scottish
souterrains are sometimes locally referred to as *weems*
(from the Gaelic *uamh*, meaning 'cave') or as *erd-houses*.

Irish souterrains are so numerous and so widespread
that it is impossible at present to classify them either
on the basis of type or distribution. Hardly a year
passes without one or more new sites being discovered.
Some Irish sites are very much more complex in plan
than those of Britain, and many contain small corbelled
side chambers.

It is probable that the majority of souterrains were
normally associated with other structures, either a
fortified site, such as Cornish forts and Irish raths, or
habitation sites. The exact relationship between a
souterrain and its associated structure is not always easy
to define without excavation. A souterrain may be
found, apparently without an associated surface structure. This is particularly true of habitation sites,
where traces of foundations may not be visible.
Similarly, there may not be any obvious surface
indications of a souterrain associated with a fortified
site or a hut circle, yet one may be found by excavation.
Many souterrains are discovered by the chance collapse

of part of the roof, either through natural causes or by ploughing or bulldozing. Yet careful examination of the area within and around a hut circle in those parts of the British Isles where souterrains are known to exist may reveal a slight linear hollow on the ground surface. This might be only a few inches deep, about 4 feet wide, but extending for 30 feet or more, and may mark the position of a souterrain.

Because of the variety of plan and size of souterrains, it is not possible to offer a simple explanation of their function. Some of the larger souterrains in Angus may have been used as cattle stalls, others were used for storage, possibly for drying meat, and it is possible that some were used as temporary refuges. Souterrains may first have been built towards the end of the Bronze Age, and some were in use in the Middle Ages, but the majority appear to date from the Iron Age (both Celtic and Roman) and the Early Christian period.

(b) *Temples*. There is no evidence that stone buildings designed for worship were in use in southern Britain before the Roman period, or elsewhere in Britain and in Ireland until the Early Christian period. The only possible exception may be the so-called Neolithic temple at Stanydale in Shetland, which resembled a large chambered cairn. Prehistoric ritual sites were normally either burial mounds, unroofed settings of standing stones (see above, page 71) or earthen enclosures (see below, page 130).

The Romans on their arrival in Britain encouraged the building of temples. Three principal types may be identified, based on the type of cult practised, classical, Romano-Celtic and eastern. It is improbable that classical temples will be discovered in the countryside, but Romano-Celtic temples are known from both town and country. The ground plan of the typical *Romano-*

Celtic temple is square, and stone foundations normally survive as two squares, one inside the other. The inner is sometimes more strongly built than the outer, as it supported the walls of a tall shrine or *cella*, whereas the outer might be of lighter construction, as it had only to support a surrounding portico. Such temples were not designed for congregational worship, but were probably repositories for cult objects, and are therefore relatively small structures, averaging about 50 feet

Fig. 31.   Romano-Celtic temple.   *Left:* Plan.
Right: Reconstruction.

square. A few temples have been identified which are either circular or polygonal in plan, but these, too, like the square temples, have inner and outer foundation courses. In the countryside Romano-Celtic temples are commonly found on hill-tops, although low-lying sites are not unknown. The occurrence on hill-tops of surface finds of Romano-British artifacts, particularly coins and parts of bronze trinkets, may lead to the identification of a temple, although there may be little or no surface indications of a structure.

Some of the larger Romano-British towns probably had communities of eastern merchants who may have built temples to their native gods. The eastern religion about which most is known in Britain is that of Mithras. A number of *mithraea* (or temples of Mithras) are known, both in town and countryside. As this was a cult restricted to men, and particularly favoured by soldiers, any new discoveries of mithraea in the countryside are likely to be made near a Roman fort. The typical *mithraeum* is rectangular in plan, with a central nave and pair of raised areas on each side, perhaps a small sanctuary built in one of the shorter end walls and an anteroom or *narthex* at the opposite end. A mithraeum was frequently built partially underground to give a cave-like effect. As membership of any single congregation was restricted to about fifty worshippers, mithraea were usually small buildings, about 50 feet long, although larger ones are known.

With the exception of Romano-Celtic temples, with their distinctive ground plan, it will normally be difficult in field work to distinguish a temple from other Romano-British structures. The chance discovery of votive offerings, altars or inscriptions on such sites may, however, suggest the existence of a ritual structure rather than, say, a villa.

(c) *Early Christian Religious Sites*. With the exception of the foundations of a possible Christian church in the Romano-British town of Silchester, near Reading, Christian churches are unknown in Roman Britain, although Christianity was practised in Britain at least from the fourth century onwards. Christianity had also penetrated beyond the Roman provinces and into Ireland during the same century. Celtic monasteries were established in Ireland and the western parts of Britain in the post-Roman period. These do not compare with the more complex medieval monasteries, but largely retained prehistoric building techniques.

Early Celtic monasteries were frequently built in remote places, such as rocky islands and remote promontories, due in part to desire of solitude for medita-

PLATE III. Broch - Dun Telve, Inverness-shire.

PLATE IV. Banks and ditches at entrance of typical multivallate hill fort.

tion. Both timber-built and stone-built monastic settlements are known to have been built, but naturally only remains of the latter have survived above ground. The monks lived in small cells, one or two to each. The cells were sometimes of dry-stone construction, often with corbelled roofs, and circular or rectangular in plan. A small church or oratory with an east–west orientation was the focal point of the monastic settlement. This, too, was often built of dry-stone walling and resembles the rectangular clochán (see above, page 100). Other buildings may have included a refectory, guest-house and *scriptorium*, where the monks worked at copying the Scriptures. Foundations of these may survive. The whole complex of buildings was enclosed within an earthwork or stone wall, sometimes that of a ring fort or disused Roman fort. It is possible, therefore, that careful field work in appropriate areas might lead to the recognition of an early monastic settlement in what might at first sight appear to be a normal type of defensive structure.

H

CHAPTER VII

Field Monuments

EARTHWORKS

In the previous three chapters we have examined some of the more important prehistoric, Romano-British and early medieval stone structures which survive in Britain and Ireland. Field survey reveals, even without excavation, considerable variety of structure and variation of plan within individual types of structure. Stone-built monuments are very durable, particularly when orthostatic slabs were used in construction and, even after disturbance, enough of a structure may survive to allow classification and perhaps sub-classification. Without excavation, grass-covered earthworks are frequently less informative, as timber was often used in construction, together with earth and sods. Excavation may reveal the ground-plan of timber-built structures and sometimes the remains of actual wood, but this will not normally be visible beforehand.

Earthworks consist of two basic components, an artificial mound and a depression, and both are easily recognised. In this chapter we may classify the more common under three headings, mounds, enclosures and linear earthworks.

MOUNDS

Two basic types of mound may be defined, burial mounds or barrows and mounds which supported a defensive structure.

(a) *Barrows.* A *barrow* is a mound of earth or chalk covering a burial. It may also cover remains of a timber structure or setting of wooden posts, but such evidence will not normally be visible in field survey. There are two basic plans, long and round.

The *long barrow* is normally Neolithic in date, and excavation shows that it usually covers the remains of a communal burial. A well-preserved site usually tapers slightly in plan from one end to the other and slopes downwards from the former. There is frequently no clear indication of the limits of the mound at the narrow end as it sometimes merges into the present ground surface. Orientation is such that the wider and higher end faces in an easterly direction, not necessarily due east, but between north-east and south-east. In appearance a long barrow sometimes resembles a partially submerged whale. Both the ends and the sides of the barrow are often curved in plan, and some smaller barrows are oval. Excavation normally reveals that such barrows were originally straight-sided. Their ratio of length to breadth is approximately 2 : 1. The length of a conventional long barrow varies between 100 and 400 feet, with the majority measuring between 100 and 200 feet. The wider end sometimes survives to a height of 6 feet or more. Many barrows built on chalk had ditches from which material for the construction of the mound was obtained. These may be identified as slight hollows running parallel with the long sides of the barrow, sometimes a short distance away from the mound. Occasionally it may be possible to trace a ditch continuing around one or both of the short ends of the barrow. The ditch may be interrupted by causeways visible on the surface.

In contrast with round barrows, which sometimes may be grouped together, long barrows are normally found singly, or occasionally in pairs. Long barrows are rarely situated on hill-tops, as round barrows often are, although they are frequently found in upland areas in chalk or limestone country. In Britain some 200 long barrows are known in Wessex, Sussex, East Anglia and on the Lincolnshire and Yorkshire Wolds. A few unchambered long mounds have been identified in eastern Scotland, but without excavation it is impossible to determine how far these Scottish mounds compare with those farther south. Unchambered long barrows appear to be unknown in Ireland.

It is possible that more long barrows await discovery, but it is less likely that any such sites will exhibit all the external features outlined above. In common with earthen round barrows, long barrows may partially or completely be denuded by ploughing. In such cases the mound may have completely disappeared or may survive to a height of only a few inches. Even such a low mound, particularly if flanked by shallow vestiges of ditches, may reveal itself to the practised eye. A completely ploughed-out long barrow may also be recognised on aerial photographs. Care should be taken in identification, as remains of a long barrow may be confused with the final traces of the bank of a hill-fort, as has happened in Gloucestershire, or two or three round barrows placed close together, movement of earth from the individual barrows having merged into an apparently homogeneous mound. A long barrow might be confused with a *pillow-mound*, a long, low mound of uncertain function, although it has been suggested that some were artificial rabbit warrens of medieval date. Long barrows might also be confused with long natural mounds of glacial debris. The possibility of confusion, however, will be reduced if a pair of flanking ditches are identified, particularly if these are wider apart at the more easterly end, if the mound has an east–west orientation, and if there is evidence that the remains of the mound both taper in width and height from east to west.

Round barrows were constructed over a wide range of time, from the Neolithic until the post-Roman period,

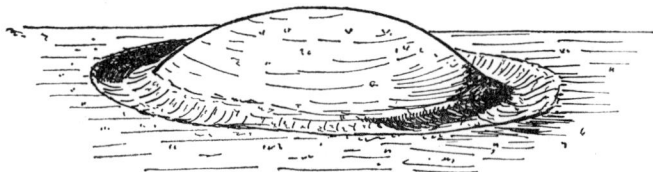

Fig. 32.

although the majority appear to date from the Bronze Age. The commonest type is the *bowl barrow*, a rounded mound, and so-called because it sometimes resembles an upturned bowl or basin. It is sometimes surrounded by a ditch, although this may be obscured by slip from the mound. Where a ditch occurs, the inner lip meets the outer edge of the mound without any intervening area of flat ground. Exceptionally there may be a small bank outside the ditch. Bowl barrows vary considerably from a diameter of 20 to 150 feet or more, and in surviving height from a few inches to 10 feet or more (Fig. 32).

Bowl barrows are very common in England, and occur on lighter soils elsewhere in Britain and in Ireland. They may be found in almost any area where fairly light soil would have provided a living for prehistoric farmers, both in upland and low-lying areas. They are less frequently found on heavier, clayey soils. Known examples of Neolithic and Iron Age round barrows belong to this class, as do Anglo-Saxon barrows, but without excavation or some knowledge of the contents of a bowl barrow it is impossible to date them. The chance find of Iron Age or Anglo-Saxon objects on the surface of a barrow does not necessarily imply that the construction of the mound dates from the Iron Age or Anglo-Saxon period, as burials of these dates may have been inserted into an already existing mound. This would be an example of *secondary burial*. Romano-British barrows are also bowl barrows, but they sometimes have external features which differ from the average Bronze Age round barrow. They tend to be large, tall and may have fairly steep sides with a somewhat flattened top, giving a slightly conical appearance. It is obviously improbable that relatively undisturbed barrows with such distinctive external features remain to be identified, but some denuded barrows which lie alongside Roman roads or near Roman villas may eventually prove to be Romano-British. Recent excavation of some presumed bowl barrows has revealed the existence of a hitherto unknown type of Romano-British burial structure.

Silbury Hill, near Avebury in Wiltshire, is a unique and impressive earthwork, and may be a giant bowl barrow. Unsuccessful attempts have been made to locate the primary burial, assuming that one exists. The mound is pre-Roman in date, and its height of 130 feet and basal diameter of 550 feet suggest that, if it is a barrow, it may contain the burial of a very important Bronze Age chieftain.

The remaining types of round barrow have a distribution more restricted in both space and time. A *bell barrow* consists of a circular mound with surrounding ditch, but, unlike the bowl barrow, which it otherwise resembles, there is a flat area of ground between the outer edge of the mound and the inner lip of the ditch. This area is known as a *berm*. A *disc barrow* consists of one or more very small burial mounds set in the centre

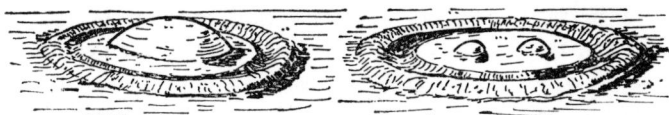

Fig. 33. *Left:* Bell barrow. *Right:* Disc barrow.

of a large flat area and surrounded by a ditch. The *bell–disc barrow* is a type intermediate between the last two. These three types may be grouped together and termed *bermed barrows*, as the berm is often a prominent feature. Where the berm is relatively narrow, how-

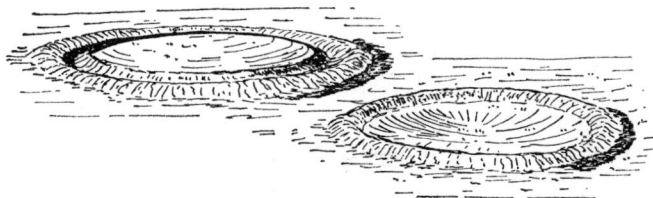

Fig. 34. *Left:* Saucer barrow. *Right:* Pond barrow.

ever, slip from the mound may have obscured it, and its true nature may be revealed only by excavation.

The *saucer barrow* consists of a very low mound, usually between 60 and 90 feet in diameter and which may originally have stood no more than 1 or 2 feet high, surrounded by a ditch, but without a berm. The *pond barrow* is really a contradiction, for, in place of a mound,

there is an artificial circular hollow, measuring between
30 and 120 feet in diameter and surrounded by a low
circular bank. Burials were inserted within the hollow
area. All three variants of bermed barrows and the
saucer barrow are frequently surrounded by a low bank
external to the ditch.

Bell, disc, bell–disc, saucer and pond barrows are
found primarily in the Wessex area of southern England,
and present evidence suggests that most date to the
Early Bronze Age. A few bell barrows have been
identified to the north, east and west of Wessex, and
there are at least two in Ireland. Beyond Wessex and
in Ireland the bowl barrow is the normal type. In
Ireland, however, and particularly in Co. Limerick,
there are numbers of *ring barrows* which resemble
Wessex saucer barrows in having a very low, circular
mound, surrounded by a ditched outer bank. They
measure between 12 and 30 feet in diameter. Sometimes the mound is absent, but the bank and ditch are
visible. Ring barrows date from the Late Neolithic
period and the Bronze Age.

Round barrows are frequently grouped together in
cemeteries, and three types have been recognised. In
the *linear cemetery* the barrows are set in a straight line,
and in the *nuclear cemetery* are grouped around a
central barrow or other structure. The *dispersed cemetery*
is a group apparently without a fixed centre. It is
common to find a concentration of barrows centred on
a henge monument. Round barrows are commonly
found on hill-tops or on false crests, so that from below
they are prominent features on the sky-line. In
Wessex and other parts of Britain groups of barrows
were frequently planted with trees in recent times to
the enhancement of the countryside, but to the detri-
ment of barrows. Many round barrows of all types

have a small central hollow.   This is usually the result
of early excavation or treasure-hunting, when a central
shaft was dug in the hope—unfortunately too often
realised—of finding the primary burial and accompanying artifacts.

It is probable that the majority of well-preserved
round barrows have been identified, although some yet
may be discovered in remote upland areas.   In areas
which have long been under cultivation barrows may
have either been reduced in height or completely
levelled by ploughing.   Such denuded sites may sometimes be recognised.   In the right lighting conditions
even the very low remains of a barrow which has been
spread by ploughing may be recognised, particularly on
newly ploughed ground.   Some features of denuded
barrows may also be revealed by growing crops.   Subsoil on the site of a former ditch has been loosened, and
therefore roots of growing crops can penetrate farther.
This means that the crop in this area will take longer
than the surrounding crop to ripen, and will therefore
appear darker in colour, often still green when the
remainder of the crop has ripened.   The crop over the
ditch will eventually grow slightly taller than the
remainder.   These colour variations in growing crops
are most easily recognised from the air (see above, page
35), but with experience they may be identified on
the ground.   Some barrows had inner cores built of
turves or sods, and covered by earth or chalk.   In chalk
country frequent ploughing may have reduced the
height of a barrow, and part of the outer envelope of
chalk will therefore have been removed, allowing roots
of growing crops to penetrate into the richer, inner core,
where they grow more strongly, as over the ditch.   In
chalk country, too, a completely ploughed-out barrow
originally built of chalk may leave traces of its former

existence in the form of a scatter of white chalk. This may be particularly noticeable in newly ploughed ground.

It may seem superfluous to be concerned with the sites of destroyed barrows, but even these may yield valuable evidence when excavated. Burials were sometimes placed on the ground surface and covered by a barrow, and so would be easily destroyed. Other burials were frequently placed in pits or graves dug into the subsoil, and these may survive after the complete destruction of the barrow. Finds may also be made in the ditch.

Relatively well-preserved barrows may sometimes be difficult of interpretation. Earthworks, by their very nature, tend to spread their limits without human interference. For this reason a ditch or a berm may not be located until after excavation. A barrow, part of which has been removed, may also remain unrecognised, although the field archaeologist will look for evidence of a ditch. More confusing, perhaps, are earthen mounds superficially indistinguishable from barrows, such as *stabilised dunes*. These were built up naturally over the centuries in sandy heathland, due to the action of wind and vegetation. Spoil heaps resulting from quarrying or the digging of a pond may resemble barrows, but the nearby presence of a pit or pond may prevent incorrect interpretation.

(b) *Defensive Mounds*. Mounds for defensive purposes were not built until the post-Roman period, but they are included here, as they may be confused sometimes with round barrows. The most distinctive defensive mound is the *motte* or *castle mound*. This is a flat-topped circular mound with relatively steep sides and surrounded by a ditch. There are considerable variations in size, and some are quite small. Many such mounds exist in England and Wales, particularly along the border between the two countries, and they are known in Scotland as far north as Aberdeenshire, and in eastern Ireland (Fig. 35).

The flat top of a motte would originally have supported a stout timber palisade surrounding a timber-built tower or *brestache*. Some towers were later rebuilt in stone and are known as *keeps*. A castle mound was frequently, although not invariably,

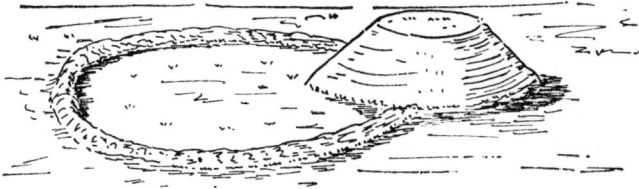

Fig. 35.

associated with a banked and ditched enclosure known as a *bailey*, built to one side of the motte. Where the remains of both motte and bailey survive, the former is unlikely to be confused with a round barrow. A denuded motte, however, sometimes loses its characteristic profile and becomes rounded. If there is no visible evidence of a bailey it may be difficult to distinguish between a barrow and a motte, although there may be clues. A motte was normally, although not always, built in a naturally defensive position, such as a natural ridge or mound, and close to water. If the site was in use over a period of years there may be evidence of an old trackway leading to it.

Whereas the great majority of mottes date from the Norman period in Britain and from the Anglo-Norman period in Ireland, in the latter country there is a second type of defensive mound which appears to have been both independent of, and earlier than, the motte. This is the *platform-type ring-fort*, in which a flat-topped mound was produced over the years by successive additions of occupation material. Excavation has shown that such sites probably existed in Ireland as early as the eighth century A.D. The platform is usually surrounded by a bank and ditch proper to a simple earthen ring-fort (see below, page 126). Absence of a bailey will normally prevent confusion with a motte.

Mottes may also be confused with glacial remains, and a small glacial moraine may even have been used as the basis of a motte. This confusion is more likely to occur in Scotland. Glacial remains are less likely to be confused with round barrows, as the latter were only exceptionally built on heavy glacial soils.

ENCLOSURES

One of the simplest methods of protecting an area of level ground is by enclosing it within a bank constructed from earth dug from a ditch. This type of earthwork has been constructed in much variety of size and defensive strength from the Neolithic to more recent times. In this section the more important prehistoric and Romano-British earthworks are defined with some reference to post-Roman earthworks, which may be confused with them. Two main types of enclosure may be defined, those built for defence and those built for ritual purposes.

(a) *Protective Enclosures*. The earliest recognised type of protective enclosure in Britain is the so-called *causewayed camp*, of which some fourteen have been identified, mainly on the chalk of Wessex and Sussex, although also on river gravels in the south of England. They date from the Neolithic period. A causewayed camp consists of one, two, three or four rings of banks and ditches enclosing an oval area. The extreme limits of such a site may measure over 1,000 feet across. Remains of banks are rarely visible today, but the silted remains of the ditches may be traced. The ditch was discontinuous, its main purpose being that of a quarry for the bank, and gaps between adjacent segments were once interpreted as causeways—hence the name, causewayed camp.

The majority of known causewayed camps are found on gently rounded hill-tops, but low-lying sites are also known on river gravels. Although usually called a 'camp', a causewayed camp is not a fortified site in the sense of a hill-fort. Sometimes they are situated in a way which does not take advantage of their hill-top position, and one of their functions appears to have been protection of livestock. They may also have served as tribal meeting-places. So far they have not been identified north of Bedfordshire, but it is possible that some may have been built in other areas of Britain where unchambered long barrows occur (see above, page 115), as both causewayed camps and long barrows were built by the same cultural group.

The main features of stone-built hill-forts have been outlined (see above, page 85) and *hill-forts* built of earth and timber, particularly when grass-covered, present similar surface features. Their grass-covered banks today are usually rounded and merge with their silted ditches. The defences of a multivallate hill-fort appear as a gently undulating series of banks and ditches, usually sloping downhill from the interior of the fort (Plate IV). Both stone-built and earth and timber forts have a similar variety of size and complexity of defences. In southern Britain earth and timber hill-forts are numerous in the Welsh Marches, Wessex and Sussex, but are strangely few in the upland areas of eastern England north of the Thames. In many cases it is not possible to determine whether or not stone was used in the construction of the defences, but reference to local geology may allow some inferences to be drawn.

The defences of the normal multivallate hill-fort are set close together and the defensive properties of a hill-top position fully appreciated. In south-west England and in south Wales a specialised form of protective enclosure was built, contemporary with more conventional hill-forts. These are *multiple-enclosure forts* or *hill-slope forts*, in which the defences, sometimes arranged concentrically, are widely spaced and form two or more enclosures. Both defences and entrances are usually slight, and the sites frequently lie on hill slopes without any tactical advantages. They are best interpreted as cattle enclosures. The focal point of such sites was a relatively small enclosure, probably containing farm buildings, and the other enclosures were arranged either concentrically with it or set alongside it. There may also be an annexe bounded by defences of similar construction.

It is unlikely that any well-preserved hill-forts remain to be discovered, but even earth and timber hill-forts, and particularly the smaller sites, may be much denuded by ploughing, so that their defences are not immediately apparent. Field work may identify some of these sites, but a careful examination of a known hill-fort may also reveal new information, such as the type of entrance. Outer banks and ditches may be recognised, and so enable a site to be properly classified as multivallate.

In Ireland the *rath* resembles the *cashel* (see above, page 93), both being ring-forts. In place of the stone-built defences of the latter the rath had an earth and timber bank and outer ditch. Some raths are multivallate with close-set defences, although there may be a level space between outer and inner defences (*berm*), and sometimes have well-protected entrances.   Like cashels, raths vary in size, but the majority were defended homesteads.

In addition to defended sites, which fall into one or other of the above categories, it is probable that, at most periods in prehistoric times from the Neolithic onwards, houses were protected by some sort of enclosing wall or fence.   Remains of homesteads in lowland areas dating from before the latter part of the Bronze Age have proved difficult to locate.   It is probable that the activities of earthworms have destroyed most of these sites, except when they may have been protected by the chance building of later structures over their remains.   Small oval or rectangular enclosures marked by low banks are known to have contained the remains of Bronze Age farms.   They have been identified on the chalk of southern England, where they are often associated with the remains of prehistoric field systems (see below, page 142), and it is possible that similar sites may be identified on lighter soils elsewhere in Britain and in Ireland.   Iron Age farmsteads were also sometimes protected by an enclosing bank and ditch.   Sites such as these which have such slight defences may be recognised from aerial photographs, but may sometimes be recognised by observation in the field.   The differential growth of crops over buried ditches, already discussed in connection with round barrows (see above, page 35), is also applicable in this context.

It is sometimes possible to identify on the ground surface traces of a trench which originally supported a wooden palisade enclosing a settlement site.   This will show as a very narrow and shallow continuous groove in the grass, and may be either single or double.   At first sight some might be confused with paths made by animals, but it is sometimes possible to trace these shallow grooves throughout their circumference. The settlement sites so enclosed are usually oval in plan and have a maximum diameter of approximately 200 feet. Sometimes the palisade was fronted by a ditch for extra protection. Although some *palisaded enclosures*, as these sites are termed, are found on hill-tops, they are also found in lower-lying positions in southern Scotland and northern England. On some hill-top sites the palisade was later replaced by a bank, converting the site into a hill-fort, although this can be established only after excavation. A stone-built bank may have been built to defend the more vulnerable side of a hill-top site, the other sides having been adequately protected by a palisade. Recognition of a palisade trench at such sites would remove the apparent anomaly of a hill-fort without defences on two or three of its sides. Surface traces of these palisade trenches have been recognised only in recent years, and particularly in northern Britain. It is not impossible that careful field work in other parts of Britain and in Ireland might reveal more, and so lead to the discovery of prehistoric habitation sites.

In the south of England a number of small rectangular earthworks have been identified which may date from the end of the Bronze Age. These, too, appear to have been cattle enclosures, as they are not strongly defended. The entrance is normally in one corner, and this distinguishes them from rectangular Roman earthworks.

During the early years of the Roman occupation of southern Britain many forts of earth and timber construction must have been built. Some were probably occupied for a short time only, perhaps for a matter of days during a campaign or while a permanent fort was being built alongside. These are known as *marching camps*, in which a tented encampment was protected by a relatively slight ditch and bank. Few of these sites are likely to be located from ground indications alone, but may be recognised on aerial photographs. In common with most Roman military sites, they have straight sides and rounded corners, but are not necessarily rectangular in plan. There are normally four or six entrances. Marching camps may vary in size; some were built by small detachments, others by whole armies.

Few Roman military sites have been identified in southern England, but remains of at least some may be discovered, whether marching camps or more permanent forts. The latter may have been occupied for a number of years and their defences were more strongly built than those of marching camps. Wooden buildings would have been built in the interior, but remains of these will be recovered only by excavation. Like marching camps, these more permanent earth and timber forts vary in size from legionary fortresses to smaller fortlets, and their size and proportions are similar to those of stone-built forts discussed in Chapter V (see above, page 95).

Roman *signal stations* were normally small earthworks, square or circular in plan, containing a tower. Several have been identified in coastal areas, particularly in Yorkshire, but many more must have existed not only in coastal areas but also inland. As in the search for any Roman military site, particular attention should be paid to the physical environment. A signal station would have had to have been visible from those on either side of it, assuming that it formed part of a system. This would suggest a preference for a hill-top site, but signal stations may also be found on lower-lying ground.

I

Roman military advance and military occupation were both carefully planned, even where, as in southern England, occupation of forts was short-lived. The Roman Army also had manuals of instruction detailing the lay-out and location of forts. In contrast with the remains of earlier periods which may be located by chance, it is sometimes possible to discover Roman military sites by deduction. For this reason, the field archaeologist who is keen to search for such sites should learn as much as possible about the Roman Army in Britain and of the lay-out of Roman roads in his area (see below, page 147). There are many parts of southern England which appear to offer considerable scope for this branch of field work.

(b) *Ritual Enclosures*. The purpose of a protective enclosure was to prevent an intruder from gaining access to the interior. An intruder might have been a large body of armed men attacking a hill-fort or a wild animal attempting to break into a stock enclosure. The purpose of earthworks surrounding a ritual site was to define the limits of the 'sacred' area. These were, perhaps, symbolic defences, a warning to those not entitled to entry to keep their distance.

As in the case of some protective enclosures, the ditch of a ritual site frequently served merely as a quarry for the bank. Although there is no strictly material reason why a ritual site should have been provided with massive banks and correspondingly wide and deep ditches, these are sometimes found surrounding henge monuments. Avebury is the outstanding example, the vertical distance from the top of the bank to the bottom of the ditch exceeding 50 feet. Unlike fortified sites, however, the ditch here lies inside the bank, a position generally unsuitable for defence.

Avebury is a *henge monument*. We have already

examined evidence for those henge monuments which incorporated stone in their structure (see above, page 73), and it will be remembered that within the bank and ditch there may have been settings of wooden posts or pits. The latter are not normally visible on the ground, but may be recognised on aerial photographs. Some of the more important henge monuments have been discovered from the air.

The distribution of henge monuments is widespread in Britain, and a few are known in Ireland. Several have been recognised in recent years, and it is possible that others remain to be discovered. They may have been greatly denuded by ploughing, but remains of a very low wide bank and shallow traces of a ditch may survive. Examination of aerial photographs may reveal crop marks which may lead to their identification on the ground (see above, page 35). Henge monuments vary considerably in size from 1,600 to 30 feet in diameter, but most possess the characteristic of an internal ditch. Some of the smaller sites belonging to class I (having single entrances, see above, page 74), were *cremation cemeteries*, dating from late Neolithic times, in which cremated remains were deposited in pits within the central area.

A large class II henge monument might be confused with a Roman *amphitheatre*, which is also oval in plan and has two opposed entrances. Remains of an amphitheatre, however, will lack an inner ditch, although there may be a marked hollow area within the bank. Amphitheatres, too, are commonly found immediately outside the walls of Romano-British towns. Remains of small henge monuments might be confused with those of a ring barrow (see above, page 120), but recognition of a gap in either bank or ditch, or in both, should remove any possible confusion. It is sometimes difficult, however, to determine without excavation whether a visible gap in an earthwork was part of the original plan or whether it has been caused in more recent times.

Other ritual enclosures which may be mentioned include *early monastic sites*. It may not always be possible to make a certain identification of such a site, but in the west of Britain and in Ireland the possibility of an enclosed site representing the remains of an early monastery should always be allowed. In place of the stone-built perimeter wall (see above, page 113), some were surrounded by earthworks. Some Romano-Celtic temples were also surrounded by small earthworks, and may yet be identified on some hill-tops.

Although enclosures bounded by banks and ditches may frequently be identified, it is often difficult to classify some. Where remains fall into one of the well-defined categories, such as hill-forts, Roman forts and henge monuments, there is little confusion, but with smaller sites of more irregular plan and where earthworks are relatively slight, a satisfactory interpretation may not be possible without excavation. This should not deter the field archaeologist from recording newly discovered sites which do not fall into one of the well-defined categories, and it is only by the patient accumulation of *data* that classification may be attempted.

Although an enclosure is unlikely to be confused with natural features, except when soil has slipped downwards on a hillside to resemble the bank of a hill-fort, some earthworks have been constructed in more recent times which might be confused with ancient structures. Remains of a medieval *moated homestead*, particularly when all traces of the superstructure have disappeared, may in England at first sight be confused with a Roman military site. Fortunately, there are several factors which should reduce the possibility of making an incorrect identification. Many moated homesteads were built in damp, low-lying areas and in positions which would not have offered the tactical advantages sought by Roman military engineers. Where the moat still holds water there is unlikely to be confusion, but a dried-up and silted moat may resemble a small Roman fort. The average moat encloses a rectangular area measuring about 200 feet by 250 feet, but the absence of both rounded corners and traces of an internal bank contrast with the surface remains of a typical Roman military site.

During the Middle Ages many earthworks were constructed to form enclosures of varying size. Those enclosing parks and other large areas are not likely to be confused with prehistoric sites, but some of the smaller ones may be. Because of their relative modernity, the banks of such sites have had less time in which to spread and therefore tend to be fairly steep-sided. Ditches tend to be less silted than the average prehistoric ditch. During the eighteenth and nineteenth centuries A.D. trees were planted on low hillocks in many parts of Britain. They were sometimes arranged in a low, oval bank, following the contour of the hill. In some places low banks have formed due to the natural action of soil creep and the accumulation of humic material, such as fallen leaves and undergrowth. The absence of a ditch and of a well-defined entrance will usually reveal the true nature of such banks.

LINEAR EARTHWORKS

Linear earthworks served to cut off or to mark the boundaries of large areas of land, frequently both linking and using the advantages of natural features such as dense woodland, swamps and rivers. Unlike those earthworks which were designed to enclose a specific area of ground, such as a hill-fort, it is improbable that the majority of linear earthworks were intended to be continuously manned in times of danger. The more massive would have served rather as frontier works, across which some control of movement might be exercised.

There are few of the more massive earthworks which may be assigned to the prehistoric period in Britain and Ireland. The most extensive, such as the Black Pig's Dyke in the north of Ireland and Offa's Dyke on the Welsh–English border, may have been influenced by memories of Roman frontier works, such as the Antonine Wall of the second century A.D., so named after the Emperor, Antoninus Pius, in whose reign it was built. The Antonine Wall, unlike Hadrian's Wall (see above, page 96), was built of turf and clay and extended through central Scotland from the Clyde to the Forth. Small earth- and timber-built forts were incorporated in the wall.

During the last century or so before the Romans conquered south-east England the Belgae constructed large earthworks. These enclosed areas so large that it is preferable to include those at St. Alban's and Colchester under the heading of linear earthworks, rather than to regard them as a low-lying equivalent of conventional hill-forts.

Most of the large-scale earthworks are more strictly linear in that they tend to run across the countryside for considerable distances. They usually consist of a single bank and ditch, and sometimes are discontinuous where swamps or dense forest would formerly have provided natural barriers. In Cambridgeshire a series of relatively short earthworks controlled access along a route which had been in use since the Neolithic period and which lay on chalk. It was bounded on each side by heavier, clayey soils, which would have supported dense forest. As far as is known, most of these date from the early post-Roman period.

In addition, less-massive linear earthworks may also be traced, particularly on the lighter soils of southern Britain. They appear to date from the Late Bronze and Early Iron Ages and possibly served as tribal boundaries or simply as boundaries of cattle ranches. They may be sometimes associated with Celtic fields (see below, page 142), settlement sites and hill-forts. In comparison with larger linear earthworks, these boundary marks are usually slight and were not defensive. In the north of England it is known that several close-set earthworks were constructed parallel to each other, and so would have provided an obstacle to cattle-raiders.

It is unlikely that field work would add much to present knowledge of the larger linear earthworks, although it might fill in some of the missing gaps. There has been much destruction of smaller linear earthworks in more recent times. Despite this, there is considerable scope for field work, allied wherever possible to the use of aerial photographs. Because of their extensive nature and the small likelihood of discovering artifacts, it is unlikely that many linear earthworks will be excavated. This means that attempts at dating and interpretation will have to be made primarily on the basis of field work. This will involve plotting their course on maps, locating missing stretches and relating them to other structures of known date. If, for example, the line of an earthwork swings round a round barrow the former was probably built later than the barrow. If a linear earthwork appears to run directly under a hill-fort it is probably earlier in date than the hill-fort.

Our present knowledge of the extent of prehistoric agriculture in Britain and Ireland is slight. Recognition and recording of linear earthworks and field systems would greatly increase this knowledge, and this is a task which offers considerable scope to the field archaeologist.

In conclusion, reference may be made to a type of linear earthwork which was constructed apparently for ritual purposes. This is the *cursus*, so named because early archaeologists likened them to Roman race tracks. A cursus consists of a parallel pair of straight banks, each with an external quarry ditch, and spaced from about 150 to 400 feet apart. They may extend over a distance of several miles, the largest known being in Dorset, with a length of six miles. One end of a cursus may be blocked by an unchambered long barrow (see above, page 115), and other long barrows may be found along its length. The exact purpose of a cursus is unknown, but the association of some with long barrows and henge monuments (see above, page 130) suggests that they may have been a type of Neolithic ritual site. They have been identified in England and Wales, mostly from aerial photographs, as being relatively slight earthworks, which have been levelled by ploughing.

CHAPTER VIII

Field Monuments

MISCELLANEOUS

THE principal types of stone structure and the more common earthworks have been examined. In this chapter we shall look at a number of miscellaneous earthworks and some stone structures. This does not imply that they are less important than, say, mounds, enclosures or linear earthworks, but they do offer certain problems of recognition and interpretation. The more important are certain types of habitation site, field systems, trackways, roads and evidence of early industry.

HABITATION SITES

In Chapter VI (see above, page 98) we saw that in many upland areas it is relatively easy to identify hut circles. Only by excavation, and possibly by aerial photography, will it normally be possible for remains of dwellings, entirely built of timber and other perishable materials, to be located. Four types of prehistoric and early historic habitation sites may be recognised in the field in the form of earthworks. Evidence of early habitation sites may also survive from the remains of cooking places.

The first of these habitation sites is the *scooped enclosure*, formed by digging out a large, level-based hollow in the edge of a terrace, normally overlooking a river or stream. This protected hollow would have contained one or more timber-built huts, the position of which may sometimes be recognised by slight hollows or stone foundations. A number of scooped enclosures are occasionally found alongside each other. It is possible that their origins date from the Roman period, but they probably continued in use into the post-Roman period. So far they have been identified primarily in the borderland between Scotland and England, particularly around the Cheviots, but field work in other areas might reveal more. At first sight they could be mistaken for small abandoned quarries. Their very recognition and interpretation are a tribute to the skill of the field archaeologist.

The second type is also confined at present to southern Scotland, but may eventually prove to have been more widespread. This is the *unenclosed platform settlement*, in which part of a hillside was also scooped out, but in this case the earth and stone so obtained was piled down the slope of the hillside to form a platform level with the area formed by the base of the scoop. This had the effect of doubling the platform area of what otherwise would have been a simple scooped enclosure. The platform is normally oval or circular in plan, with a diameter of between 25 and 80 feet. Each platform probably contained a round timber-built hut. Like scooped enclosures, unenclosed platform settlements may occur in groups, set side by side along the contour of a hill and, rarely, one above the other. They, too, resemble abandoned quarries, but the presence of a deliberately built platform will normally prevent an incorrect interpretation. Excavation suggests that their origins date from the Iron Age.

Both types resemble a later type of *platform house*

found in Wales, particularly in the north of the country, and apparently dating from the Middle Ages. A level area, usually rectangular in plan, was excavated into a hillside. Some of the spoil was used to build a protective bank around the upper part of the scoop. The buildings associated with this type of platform are normally rectangular. Traces of cattle enclosures and old field boundaries may sometimes be recognised near by. Recognition of scooped enclosures of differing dates in two different parts of Britain and their superficial similarity to disused hillside quarries suggest that similar sites may yet be identified in other parts of Britain, and possibly in Ireland.

The fourth type is the *crannog*, usually an artificial island in a lake, river estuary, bog or marsh, and which normally supported a single homestead. Larger groupings of structures are also known, such as the *lake villages* of Somerset, which are now known to have been built on the surface of a raised bog in a manner similar to that of the more conventional crannog. An artificial island was formed of layers of timber, brushwood, bracken, peat and stones. Pointed stakes were often driven into the subsoil around the perimeter as a palisade, and stakes were also driven vertically into the main mass of the crannog for stability. There was frequently a narrow artificial causeway joining the crannog to the shore. Crannogs were built for protection, and range in date from the Iron Age to the Middle Ages.

The present appearance of a crannog may vary considerably. The most obvious is an immediately recognisable artificial island lying a short distance from the shore of a lake. It will often have trees growing on it. Crannogs have sometimes been first recognised by a lowering of the water level of a lake, either deliberately or during a drought. Others may appear today as small islands in marshy or boggy land. Crannogs have also been recognised in areas which, because of intensive drainage over the centuries, are no longer damp, and which are indistinguishable from the surrounding countryside. Sites have been recognised by remains of worked timber found on their surface. Crannogs are of particular importance, as artifacts made of normally perishable substances, such as wood and leather, bone and even textiles, often survive and may be recovered by excavation.

The field archaeologist should therefore take particular notice if lakes or marshy land in his area are to be partially or completely drained. Similarly, a careful watch should be kept in periods of prolonged drought. Should the site of a possible crannog be identified, it should be carefully examined, as in the past many finds of considerable importance have been found lying on the surface. Any such discoveries should *immediately* be reported to one of the national or local museums, or the secretary of the local archaeological society. More than 200 crannogs have been identified in Ireland, particularly in the west and north-west and in Co. Antrim, and rather fewer in Britain, and it is probable that more await discovery.

Evidence of human occupation is also provided by remains of *ancient cooking places*, formed of mounds of small burnt stones and charcoal, and usually found on the shore of a lake or river bank or close to a stream. They are common in the south and west of Ireland, where they are variously known as *fulacht fees* or *deer roasts* (from the Irish, *fulacht fiadh*) and *fulacht fians* (from the Irish, *fulacht fiann*). Fewer have been recognised in Britain, although some are known in north Wales. A well-preserved mound of this type is often horse-shoe shaped in plan, although it may have a more irregular plan. The mound itself is composed of discarded and broken stones which, having been heated in the fire, were dropped into a cooking-vessel to bring water to the boil. The vessel was frequently a wooden trough set into the ground, and remains of some have survived. It lay alongside the hearth where the stones were heated. The latter are sometimes termed *pot-boilers*. Both the hearth and cooking-trough usually lay within the hollow of a horse-shoe mound, when the latter was of that shape. Some sites also had, in addition to the cooking-trough, a stone-lined pit in which meat was roasted.

As so few open-air cooking places have been excavated, it is not possible to date them closely. Present evidence suggests that their use dates back at least to the Bronze Age and continued into the Middle Ages.

The method of cooking which was practised was simple but efficient and, until the widespread use of metal cooking vessels, was perhaps in common use. The archaeological significance of open-air cooking places lies in the opportunity they may offer for the location of habitation sites. Many of the mounds are small, but larger mounds up to 80 feet in diameter have been identified. This may suggest continuous occupation in the vicinity over a period of time and, if so, remains of a house site may survive. A small timber-built hut was found during the excavation of one *fulacht fiadh* in Ireland. The distinguishing features to be looked for in the mound are traces of burning and fire-shattered stones or pebbles. The site will normally lie close to a convenient water supply.

Any scatter of fire-shattered stones on the ground surface should be examined. Some may lead to remains of prehistoric habitation sites, as pot-boilers appear to have been in common use from the Neolithic onwards. As their name suggests, they were used to heat pots of water as well as the larger wooden troughs of the cooking places. Such scatters, however, may be deceptive, as stones may be burnt and shattered by heath fires and the like.

FIELD SYSTEMS

Reference has also been made to various enclosures which were apparently used in prehistoric times for herding cattle and other animals (see above, page 126). In this section we may examine the little surviving evidence for arable farming which may be recognised in the field.

The earliest farmers coming into Britain and Ireland probably did not possess knowledge of the plough, but successfully cultivated the ground with hoes or digging sticks. Traces of such small plots will clearly be difficult to locate, even if any have survived. With the introduction of the plough during the Bronze Age, recognisable field systems came into being.

As the earliest known type of plough used in Britain was capable only of scratching the surface, and not turning the sod, it was necessary to cross plough. This tended to produce fields which were approximately square in plan and which varied in size from about one-quarter of an acre to two acres in area. These are commonly known as *Celtic fields*, although it is now known that the earliest date from a period before the Celts arrived in Britain. In the south of England at least, Celtic fields were in use from the Bronze Age to the post-Roman period, a period in excess of 1,000 years. During the Roman period traditional farming methods remained in use alongside larger villa estates.

Although the boundaries of such fields may sometimes be identified either on the ground or from aerial
photographs, they were not enclosed in the manner
of modern fields by hedges or stone walls. Their limits
were defined either by low banks of earth or low mounds
of stone. From the Bronze Age onwards gently sloping
areas of light soil, particularly on the chalk of Sussex
and Wessex, were ploughed. This caused a slight
movement of disturbed soil, known as *soil creep*. Movement ceased at the lower limits of the ploughed area

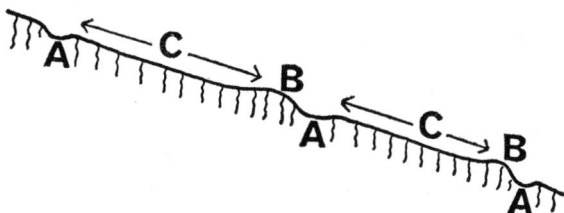

Fig. 36. A—negative lynchet; B—positive lynchet;
C—ploughed area.

and gradually accumulated in a small, low, rounded
bank, known as a *lynchet* or *positive lynchet*. At the
upper limit of the ploughed area a slight hollow
developed, caused by the displacement of soil. This
hollow is termed a *negative lynchet*. Slight, but broad
banks also formed at each side of the field, which were
undisturbed by the plough and so were unaffected by
soil creep.

It was normal for Celtic fields to be grouped together
in *field systems*, forming a kind of rough chequer-board
pattern. In upland areas of light soils which have
remained undisturbed by later agriculture Celtic fields
may still be identified. It will be appreciated that
lynchets are very slight earthworks, and it has long been
recognised that the best time to view them is either early

in the morning or late in the afternoon of a sunny day when the sun is low in the sky. The pattern of lynchets is then emphasised by their shadows. A field system may sometimes be viewed to advantage from a piece of high ground overlooking it and, of course, from aerial photographs. In this way the pattern as a whole may be studied in a manner not normally possible at ground level. Where surface indications have been obliterated by later agriculture a pattern of banks and ditches may appear in favourable conditions on aerial photographs. It is becoming increasingly apparent that light soils in low-lying positions, particularly gravels, were also cultivated.

In more stony regions, particularly in northern England, low banks of stone may form the limits of fields. These banks were built from stones removed from the surface of the field. Some ancient field systems in northern Britain are associated with *clearance cairns*, small mounds formed by collecting stones from the surface of the field (see above, page 70). Groups of several clearance cairns may be found together near the limits of cultivated ground, and their presence may lead to the identification of field systems. Stone banks forming field boundaries may often be obscured by vegetation, and there is therefore considerable scope in upland areas for the field archaeologist in identifying and plotting them. It is known that crops were grown from the Neolithic onwards, even in upland areas, as shown by impressions of cultivated grain which have been found on pottery. There is little detailed knowledge yet about the field systems themselves. Many of these may be covered by peat, and extensive peat cutting should be followed by field observation.

Field systems form one source of evidence for early occupation, as they are sometimes associated with farmsteads.   On lighter soils the latter will normally appear as small circular or rectangular earthworks which originally contained timber-built houses or huts (see above, page 127).   A complex of fields and settlement sites may also have been associated with cattle enclosures, perhaps also surviving as earthworks, and trackways (see below, page 146).   In some areas they appear to have been associated with hill-forts.   In stony areas stone-built enclosures and hut circles may also be identified in association with field systems. The discovery of one type of remains may lead to another, and the field archaeologist should not restrict himself to looking for one particular type of field monument to the exclusion of others.   In looking for traces of ancient fields one should always look for habitation sites, and vice versa.   This is particularly important, as we have so little evidence of prehistoric settlement sites as compared with ritual sites.

It has been suggested that the Belgae, who dominated south-east England during the century before the Roman occupation, introduced a heavier plough which was capable of turning the sod.   If this were so, it would be difficult in the field to distinguish remains of Belgic agriculture from those of the Anglo-Saxons, who initiated on a large scale the cultivation of heavier, low-lying soils which has continued unbroken to the present.   The major reason for the survival of some Celtic fields is that they have not been ploughed since the light plough went out of use in their particular area. As the heavier plough turned the sod, cross ploughing was unnecessary, and the familiar pattern of long strips of ploughed ground, sometimes separated by low banks or furrows, was produced.

K

TRACKWAYS AND ROADS

(a) *Trackways.* Roads having a made surface and of regular width in the modern manner are unknown in Britain prior to the Roman period. It is therefore difficult to identify with any certainty trackways which may have been used in prehistoric times. From the Neolithic period onwards there was a considerable amount of trade in raw materials and finished articles, and much of this appears to have followed certain well-defined routes. A good deal of the heavier, bulky material was undoubtedly carried by water, and it is sometimes forgotten that many parts of Britain and Ireland are provided with extensive natural waterways which would have been suitable for the dug-out canoes known to have been in use at the time. Even so, over-land travel would also have been necessary. In the earlier periods this was probably on foot, human or animal, but the wheel was known in Europe from the Bronze Age onwards, although to what extent carts and the like were in use in Britain and Ireland at that time is unknown. Certainly by the Iron Age there is clear evidence of the use of wheeled vehicles.

We have seen that wherever possible prehistoric man avoided living on heavier, wooded soils. In the same way, when travelling, he appears to have kept to open country. This would normally have led him to choose routes along upland ridges, particularly along the downs of southern Britain, which was well provided with a network of natural routes along the ridgeways radiating from the Wessex area.

Having defined the general lines of possible pre-historic routes, it would be impossible to pinpoint the actual line of a trackway. The line of the Icknield Way, running from East Anglia to Wessex, is generally accepted as having been in use from prehistoric times, but its route may be defined only in general terms. Without a prepared surface a trackway would become impassable in wet weather, and travellers would tend to avoid the muddier sections and ruts by moving on to adjacent ground. In time this might develop into a strip several hundred yards wide.

Where natural features restricted this spread *hollow ways* might develop. They were caused by constant traffic wearing away the ground surface into hollows, which may sometimes be identified on the ground or on aerial photographs. Local trackways may more easily be traced among field systems, where they sometimes survive as hollow ways linking settlement sites with fields and cattle-enclosures. These relatively shallow hollow ways should not be confused with the deeper ones which are in use today, and which are of much more recent formation.

Although there is no evidence for metalled road surfaces dating from prehistoric times, carefully constructed trackways were in use in Britain and Ireland from the Bronze Age onwards. These will be visible to the field worker only in exceptional circumstances, as they were constructed from timber and brushwood to form causeways across swampy ground. Few of these have been accurately plotted, and they should be looked for in areas where peat is being cut. Even if only a short section is found, an accurate record of its dimensions and position may subsequently be correlated with further discoveries.

(b) *Roads*. In this section we are concerned only with Roman roads. Much is known and has been written on this subject, yet many problems remain. The precise routes of the major roads radiating from London, such as those now known as Watling Street and Ermine Street, and the Foss Way, which runs across England from Devon to Lincolnshire, are known for much of their length. A glance at the most recent edition of the Ordnance Survey's *Map of Roman Britain* (see above, page 34), however, shows that there are stretches of these and other major roads which have not yet been plotted with absolute certainty. There are many stretches of minor road which have not yet been identified, and roads which probably led to a number of Romano-British sites remain equally unknown.

A well-known characteristic of major Roman roads in flat or gently undulating countryside is their tendency to lie in straight sections, sometimes extending over several miles, and accurately aligned between two visible points on the horizon. Wherever possible, this lay-out was attempted in more hilly country, but where a slope was too excessive for wheeled traffic, the road was laid out in a series of zig-zags to reduce the gradient. Where natural obstacles, such as dense forest or swamp, intervened a road may have taken a detour around them. In general, however, Roman military engineers attempted wherever possible to lay out the line of their roads in straight lines.

Roman roads were well constructed. This is particularly true of major roads, many of which were built initially for military purposes. Many continued to serve as the main routes along which supplies were brought to forts and, as they were also in constant use by Roman officials, they were well maintained. Most minor roads, too, were carefully constructed, although some were narrower than major roads. Material used in construction varied according to local materials available, but there was normally a cambered and metalled surface of flint, gravel or other stone, bounded on each side by a kerb of larger stones. This lay on top of a sandwich of stone and earth, which in turn often rested on a foundation of heavier blocks of stone. This method of construction assisted drainage, and this was further helped by a ditch dug on each side of the road. The flanking ditches of major roads sometimes lay a short distance away from the road surface, perhaps as much as 80 feet apart, although the average width between ditches was about 20 feet. The metalled surface was often about 17 feet wide.

Very few stretches of surfaced Roman road are visible today in Britain. Many stretches have been built over by roads of more recent date, others have been robbed for building material and others have disappeared under the plough. In some places the line of a road may be traced by its silted ditches. Where major roads crossed marshy ground, and sometimes even in well-drained countryside, they were built on an *agger*, a broad low bank or causeway, and stretches of agger sometimes survive. An agger running across open country may be easy to recognise, but as Roman roads were not infrequently used in later times as boundaries, an agger may be hidden under the line of a hedge. Aggers hidden in this way have been identified because on slightly sloping ground they may have destroyed the natural drainage, so that water, in the form of a pond or swamp, accumulated on the uphill side. When the road was in use, of course, drainage was provided artificially by culverts, but after the road ceased to be maintained the culverts became blocked.

The line of a road may also be traced on aerial photographs. On arable land the position of a road may be identified, even although there may not be traces of either agger or ditches. A road which has become completely buried through centuries of ploughing may reveal its presence by a scatter of small stones lying on the surface of a newly ploughed field in an area which is not otherwise stony. This stone represents material which originally formed part of the road and which has been scattered during ploughing. Any such scatter should be examined carefully and should be traced for a considerable distance before it may be accepted as evidence for the line of a road. A more localised scatter might result from buried foundations. Where a Roman road was built on a fairly steep slope, it may have formed a kind of zigzag hollow way, and recognition of this might lead to the recognition of a continuation of the same road on nearby level ground.

In addition to remains of roads which are immediately visible either in the field or on aerial photographs, documentary evidence may help to locate missing stretches. In the Anglo-Saxon period and later the line of a Roman road was frequently used as a boundary between counties, parishes and estates. The more obvious boundaries have been examined in the search for missing stretches of Roman road, but it is possible that reference to this source, particularly to local estate maps and early land charters, may help in the identification of minor roads.

Remains of newly discovered roads which have provisionally been identified as Roman should be tested by excavation. In some cases the method of construction will tend to support such an identification. In the absence of datable finds, which will only rarely be made, it may be difficult to prove that a road is Roman in date. Any new identification must take into account all available evidence. The complete line of a road may be plotted only after a good deal of field work has identified a number of short stretches. In general, any new discoveries of possible Roman road should fit into the known pattern. That is, they should be aligned on known or suspected Romano-British features, buildings or road junctions, and not normally stand in isolation. Apparently isolated stretches may be identified, and they should be regarded as only provisionally Roman in date until further evidence is available to enable a decision to be made one way or the other. One final word—in tracking Roman roads it is important to use a large-scale map. The 2½-inch Ordnance Survey map is ideal for this purpose (see above, page 20).

EARLY INDUSTRIAL SITES

In prehistoric times the average community was self-sufficient in that it produced most of its own manufactured goods, such as pottery. From the Neolithic, however, there is considerable evidence in Britain and Ireland that the raw materials from which axe-heads were made were exploited on what today we should call an industrial scale. More than twenty sites where the preliminary working of stone axe-heads was carried on have been identified mainly in Britain, but including two sites in Ireland. These sites are known as *axe factories*, and may be identified by scatters of worked and broken stone lying among scree on some hillsides in northern and western Britain and in Ireland. *Rough-outs* may also be found. These are unfinished axe-heads which have been worked by flaking suitable pieces of hard, fine-grained rock into the approximate shape of a stone axe-head. The final polishing was apparently not carried on at the axe factory itself.

By examining a small sample of the rock from which an axe-head was made, geologists are able to identify its source. From this it has been shown that axe-heads were traded over considerable distances. Axe-heads made in the Lake District and north Wales, for example, have been found in some numbers in the south of England, and axe-heads made in Co. Antrim were even carried across the Irish Sea to Britain. It is hoped eventually to examine all axe-heads in Britain and Ireland in an attempt to locate the source of their raw material. This is, of course, largely a specialised task for geologists, but it is probable that the sites of more axe factories remain to be discovered by field archaeologists. So far there has been little of this work in Scotland, but the widespread distribution of axe-heads makes it seem likely that more axe factories will be discovered in that country, particularly as there are many outcrops of suitable rock. This is a task to which the field archaeologist may contribute, but before doing so he should familiarise himself with the appearance both of complete and broken rough-outs and of the waste flakes produced during manufacture.

Flint was also used for the manufacture of axe-heads and other tools. There is considerable evidence for its large-scale exploitation in the flint mines of southern and eastern England. The *flint mine* was a true mine, in that shafts were sunk into the chalk and frequently interconnected by series of underground galleries. Neolithic man had apparently come to appreciate that flint freshly mined from the chalk produced tools and weapons of better quality than that found in surface outcrops.

As flint extracted from one part of the mine became exhausted it was customary to fill-in abandoned shafts, and these may be recognised on the ground surface. A number of filled-in shafts are normally found close together, and surface indications may extend over several acres. There will also be numbers of mounds,

composed of chalk extracted from shafts and galleries.
All this may resemble the aftermath of quarrying which
might date from more recent times. There is evidence,
however, that in addition to mining, flint was sometimes worked on the surface near the mines themselves.
Useless protuberances occurring on freshly mined
nodules were frequently struck off and abandoned
at the site and some of the crust or *cortex* of the
flint removed. The site of a mine may therefore be
identified, as in the case of an axe-factory site, by the
presence on the ground surface of quantities of waste
material.

From the Bronze Age onwards metals, such as
copper, tin and gold, were extracted and worked in
considerable quantities in various parts of Britain and
Ireland. Iron was added during the Iron Age. Little
is known of prehistoric methods of extraction, but the
field archaeologist should be familiar with the location
of metal deposits which are known or thought to have
been worked during that period. Surface finds of
artifacts and waste products in the form of slag and
burning may eventually lead to the discovery of prehistoric smelting and casting furnaces.

Most prehistoric communities made their own
pottery, which does not appear to have been produced
in Britain on an industrial scale until the Roman
period. The site of a pottery kiln may be identified
by quantities of *wasters*, sherds of broken and mis-
shaped pots which were rejected after firing by potters.
There may also be considerable evidence of burning,
perhaps including charcoal. Traces of the kiln structure itself may survive, but this will normally be
recovered only after excavation. Several Romano-
British kilns have been found and more may be discovered during ploughing, digging and bulldozing.

At least one prehistoric potter's workshop has been found in Britain, and it is possible that, despite the small scale of production, others may yet be recovered. Such a discovery might also lead to the location of a prehistoric occupation site.

CHAPTER IX

Casual Finds of Artifacts

WE have seen that the position of certain buried sites, such as Roman villas or Romano-British temples, may be located by a surface scatter of broken pottery, bone or metal. In this chapter we are concerned with the various types of artifacts which may be found by chance on the ground surface or in ground newly disturbed either by man or nature. There are many parts of Britain and Ireland, for example, where prehistoric flint artifacts may still be found lying on the surface. Many more come to light every year as a result of ploughing, particularly deep ploughing, during peat cutting, quarrying, the digging of trenches for water, gas or electricity pipes and cables, on building sites and so on. Shifting sand, collapse of river banks, coastal erosion and many other natural agencies may also reveal artifacts. Artifacts discovered by any of these means may vary considerably, both in condition and range of type. Some may be complete and in a good state of preservation. These are normally easy to recognise. Others may be broken or in a poor state of preservation, and so may be difficult to recognise. The great majority found will have little monetary value, others may be very valuable, particularly if made of gold or silver. All finds, however, whether complete or broken, have a potentially high archaeological value and should be reported to a museum (see below, page 190).

Because of the very wide range of artifacts which might be found, it is impossible in a single chapter to describe each type in detail. To do so would need a separate book considerably longer than this! In any case, drawings and photographs are imperfect substitutes for looking at—and preferably handling—actual objects. This may best be done in a museum, and the field archaeologist should lose no opportunity of visiting museums to memorise not only the shape but also the texture of different types of artifacts. Drawings and photographs, of course, have their uses, particularly in communicating knowledge of finds by publication in books and journals. Experience quickly teaches us how to visualise the actual appearance of an artifact from drawings or photographs. An initial difficulty may be the ability to visualise the size of an artifact from published drawings or photographs when the latter are reproduced at a scale different from that of the artifact itself. A drawing of a pot or flint implement reproduced at one-quarter of the original size may give a false impression of true size to the beginner. This difficulty should be mastered as soon as possible. It is very difficult to reproduce the texture of an object on paper. This is particularly true of pottery, the texture of which is often an important diagnostic feature.

In this chapter we shall examine some of the main types of prehistoric and Romano-British artifacts which may be found in Britain and Ireland. These may be considered under four main headings; stone, pottery, metal and perishable substances.

STONE

(a) *Flint and Chert*.   For the greater part of Prehistory stone was the most common raw material used for the manufacture of tools and weapons and, even after the introduction of metal, stone tools continued to be used. Flint, above all, was preferred, as its properties allowed relatively rapid ease of working and the production of a sharp point or cutting edge.   Chert, which has similar properties, was also widely used.   These properties appear to have been appreciated and made use of by early man from the beginning of the Palaeolithic period.   Flint also had the advantage of being found in many parts of these islands, normally in chalk, but it also occurred as beach pebbles.   The casual find of a flint flake, as opposed to a recognisable type of artifact, in an area such as Wessex or Co. Antrim, where flint is found naturally in considerable quantities, may have no archaeological significance.   If flint flakes are found in areas far away from natural flint-bearing areas, and particularly if they are found in quantity within a restricted area, their discovery should be noted, as they may lead to the location of a prehistoric site.

The physical appearance of flint cannot be adequately described or illustrated, but once it has been seen its appearance is not easily forgotten.   In general, it is a glass-like substance which varies in its degree of trans-lucence and colour according to its source.   Much of it is honey-coloured, but colour may range through white and various shades of grey to black.   Some is transparent, some opaque.   Chert is generally similar, although a little coarser in texture.   It is most com-monly dark grey or black in colour and usually opaque.

A flint is said to have been *worked* when numbers of small flakes have been removed from its surface to leave

small shallow depressions. With a recognisable artifact, such as an arrowhead or scraper, there is little
doubt that the surface has been worked by man, but
flint may also be flaked by a variety of natural agencies.
Many museums have exhibitions showing the properties
of flint and examples of different techniques of working
the substance. Wherever possible, these should be
studied. Until this has been achieved, it will be useful
to study one of the books listed below which discuss
flint working (see below, page 202).

A very wide range of flint types may be found in
England and Wales which range in date from the
earlier part of the Palaeolithic onwards. At present
there is no certain evidence of Palaeolithic artifacts
having been found in either Scotland or Ireland. It
must be remembered that at times during the Palaeolithic period only part of southern England would have
been left uncovered by ice sheets which spread south-
wards during the so-called 'ice-ages'. This means that
areas in which Palaeolithic artifacts are likely to occur
are limited. It is also important to appreciate that
artifacts of this period, more so than those of later
periods, may today be found some distance away from
the place where they originated. During the many
thousand years of the Palaeolithic period and the ten
thousand years since it ended rivers have changed their
courses, and much soil and stone has been moved and
deposited elsewhere by water and ice action. This is
particularly true of river gravels, in which Palaeolithic
artifacts are frequently found. These, too, were often
carried considerable distances. Gravel has frequently
been used in more recent times in road building and as
ballast. Artifacts may be carried in this material and
deposited some distance away. A detailed note of the
circumstances in which flint artifacts are found should

be made. This also applies to all casual finds, but to Palaeolithic flint artifacts in particular.

One of the most common and distinctive of Palaeolithic flint artifacts is the *hand axe* (Fig. 37). This was a heavy, all-purpose tool made from a large core of flint and which would have been useful for skinning large animals, for chopping and cutting and for grubbing up roots. There are several varieties, but the typical hand

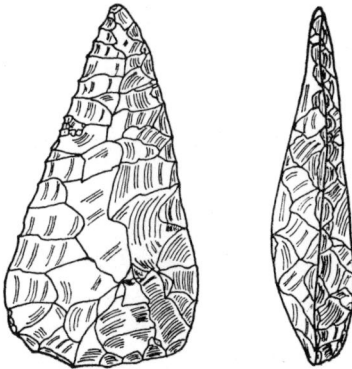

Fig. 37.

axe is roughly pear-shaped with a narrow tip and heavy rounded or flattened base. It tends to be lozenge-shaped in cross-section, wide near the base and becoming narrower towards the tip. Other Palaeolithic tools which may be found in southern Britain range from crudely worked flints, which are difficult to distinguish from naturally flaked flint and known as *eoliths*, to well-made scrapers and knives.

Towards the latter part of the Palaeolithic there was a tendency for flint artifacts to be reduced in size. This tendency was maintained during the succeeding Mesolithic period, when the microlith was produced in large quantities. A *microlith* is simply a very small worked flint, having either a sharp point or cutting edge, or both, and often a blunted back. It may be no longer than the nail of one's little finger in length, but yet will show signs of skilful working. Microliths were used in composite tools and weapons, in which a number of microliths were mounted in bone or wooden handles or hafts to act as the cutting edge of a knife or as missile points and barbs. Microliths may be divided into two main types, *geometric microliths*, which were flaked into well-defined shapes such as trapezes and

Fig. 38.

crescents, and *non-geometric microliths*, which are less easy to classify by shape (Fig. 38).

Considerable numbers of microliths may sometimes be found in sandy areas, particularly in upland country such as the Pennines. Many of their users were hunters who preferred to live away from forests, and so had little need of heavier, wood-working tools. During the Mesolithic, however, the axe (as opposed to the hand axe, which is not strictly an axe) was invented. Mesolithic axe-heads may be found in damper, low-lying areas, often in association with microliths. Mesolithic axe-heads vary in size from a few inches to more than one foot in length. Unlike Neolithic axe-heads, their surfaces were not polished.

Although farming was introduced into Britain and Ireland during the Neolithic, hunting continued to be important and arrowheads of that period are frequently found. Unlike many artifacts of the preceding periods, they are immediately recognisable, if unbroken. The most typical are leaf- and lozenge-shaped. These classifications are descriptive and self-explanatory. The *leaf-shaped arrowhead* usually has a rounded base tapering upwards to the point and commonly resembles the outline of a laurel or willow leaf. Lozenge-shaped arrowheads are somewhat similar, but have an outline more angular than that of the former. Both types may measure less than one inch in length, although some exceed this. They normally have a flattened cross-section, measuring one-twelfth of an inch or less in

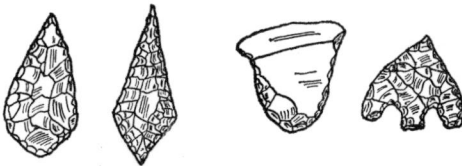

Fig. 39. Neolithic and Early Bronze Age flint arrowheads.

thickness, and are usually worked on both faces. Flint *javelin-heads* of the same general outlines were also made and may measure three inches or more in length. The faces of some lozenge-shaped javelin-heads found in Ireland are sometimes ground and polished. A third relatively common type of Neolithic arrowhead is the *chisel-ended arrowhead*, which is trapezoidal or triangular in outline. The sharp, chisel-like edge was used instead of the point, and was used probably for shooting birds and small game to lessen the danger of damaging the flesh. In addition, triangular and 'lop-sided' arrowheads may also be found, the latter having a single barb-like protuberance on one side only.

Knives and scrapers were also produced in quantity during the Neolithic, but it is often difficult to date casual finds accurately, as design sometimes changed

L

little from one period to the next. A distinctive Neo-lithic type, found mainly in Ireland, is the *hollow scraper*, in which the working edge has a marked concave outline. One specialised knife-like object which appeared during the Neolithic was the *sickle blade*. This was a large flint knife, measuring five or more inches in length, and usually either rectangular or slightly crescentic in outline. The cutting edge may have a distinctive sheen or gloss caused by cutting the stalks

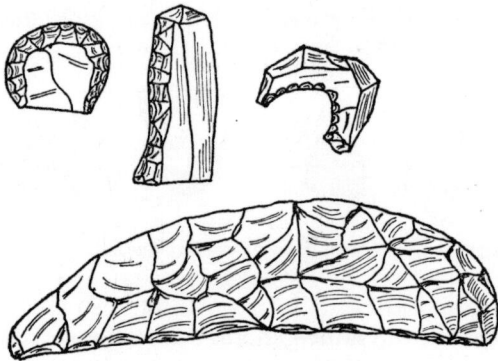

Fig. 40. *Upper:* flint scrapers. *Lower:* sickle blade.

of grasses. Sickle blades were normally mounted in bone or wooden handles, but it is unlikely that the latter will survive as casual finds, unless found in water-logged conditions.

Neolithic axe-heads differ from those of the Meso-lithic in having a more regular outline and cross-section. The latter is usually oval. Most are polished, either at their cutting edge only or over the whole surface. This polishing normally removes all traces of flaking, and the resultant surface is quite smooth and, in the finest examples, glass-like.

At the beginning of the Bronze Age a new type of

arrowhead gradually replaced Neolithic types. This
was the *barbed-and-tanged arrowhead*, which has a central
tang for attachment to the shaft and a pair of flanking
barbs. The sides are slightly convex in outline, and
their shape is best appreciated by reference to Fig.
39. This type of arrowhead is commonly associated
with Beaker pottery, but casual surface finds are not
uncommon. A more elegant version may be found,
mainly in southern England, where they appear to be

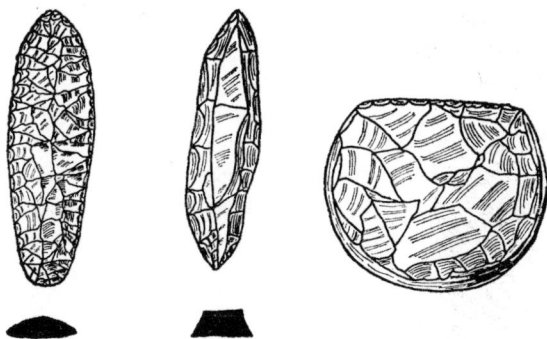

Fig. 41. Slug knife, fabricator and discoidal knife.

associated particularly with the Wessex area. This
type tends to be larger than the simple barbed-and-
tanged arrowhead and is distinguished by its very fine
flint working and the careful finish of the barbs and
tang, so that all three have straight edges in line with
each other. Elongated arrowheads and javelin-heads,
some barbed-and-tanged and others with tangs only,
are commonly found in Ireland. Like *hollow* based
arrowheads, which are barbed but not tanged, they
are difficult to date, but are most likely to belong to the
Bronze Age.

The *plano-convex knife*, sometimes called the *slug knife*, dates from the earlier part of the Bronze Age. It has parallel sides and rounded ends. One face is flat and unworked; the other is rounded and worked, and the knife is approximately D-shaped in cross-section. The *fabricator*, too, dates from approximately the same period, and one surface is similarly unworked or has limited working. The opposite face is more angular than that of the plano-convex knife and is ridge-shaped in cross-section. The sides taper towards the tips, and these sometimes show signs of bruising. It is thought that these tools were used in flint working or in 'fabricating' flint tools, hence the name *fabricator*. Both types usually measure about three inches or so in length. The *discoidal knife* appears to have originated in late Neolithic times, but continued in use into the Early Bronze Age. It is approximately circular in outline, with a thin, flattened cross-section. Its surface is carefully worked to produce a sharp cutting edge around the circumference.

In addition to flint types listed in this section, many others were produced during the prehistoric period, and more particularly during the Palaeolithic. It requires some detailed knowledge and experience of handling flint artifacts before this variety can be mastered and the various types classified according to cultures. This knowledge is not difficult to acquire, but consideration of it is beyond the scope of this book. Reference has been made to eoliths (see above, page 159), and the problem of their interpretation is one which primarily concerns students of the early part of the Palaeolithic. It must be remembered, however, that flint may have been flaked and worked in the form of a very rough knife or scraper for one single task, such as sharpening a piece of wood, and immediately discarded. Such a flint would strictly be an artifact, but would be impossible to classify. If found in isolation it would probably be unrecognised as an artifact. As we have seen, casual finds of flint in areas far from sources of the raw material may have some archaeological significance, and their position should be recorded.

As far as the field archaeologist is concerned, he should learn to recognise flint as a substance in all its variety of colour and texture. Most important of all, all finds and the circumstances of their discovery should be reported to a museum.

(b) *Other Stone Artifacts*. The oldest artifacts made from stone other than flint likely to be found in the British Isles date from the Mesolithic. Rounded pebbles were perforated so that they might be mounted on wooden shafts as hammers. These normally have *hour-glass perforations*, which were produced by boring with a drill having a pointed bit, so that two V-shaped hollows drilled from opposite sides met near the centre (Fig. 42 *top left*). Similar pebbles had small hollows pocked on each side to act as thumb and finger grips.

Neolithic polished *stone axe-heads* made from a variety of rocks are frequently found. There is also some variety of shape and size, but most approximate to those of flint axe-heads (Fig. 42 *right*). Most stone axe-heads are polished all over their surface, but unfinished axe-heads, rough-outs from axe factories (see above, page 151), may be found. Stone balls, about the size of a tennis ball, were decorated all over their surfaces with carved motives, including spirals, discs and small bosses. They have been found principally in north-east Scotland as casual finds, and appear to be Neolithic in date.

At the beginning of the Bronze Age perforated stone *axe-hammers* appeared approximately contemporary with the arrival of Beaker pottery. These hammers normally have cylindrical perforations produced by a

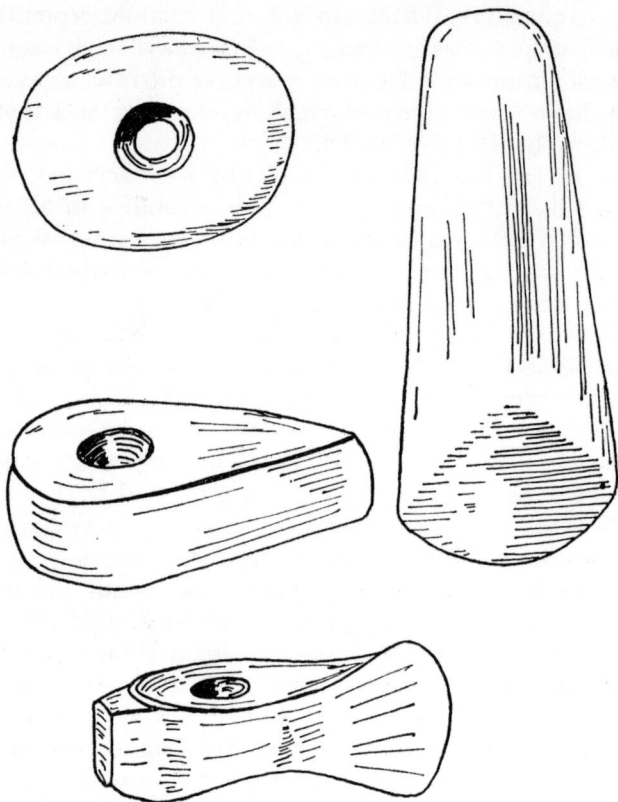

Fig. 42.

hollow drill. They have a simple outline with a flat upper and lower surface and a rounded butt which widens before tapering to the tip. The perforation is normally at the widest part of the object (Fig. 42 *centre*). *Battle-axes* also date from the earlier part of the Bronze Age in Britain and Ireland. They are perforated and vary considerably in size and outline (Fig. 42 *lower*). Most have splayed cutting edges, often at both ends, and some are ornamented with grooves and ridges. A type of large, heavy *hammerhead* also appears to date from the Bronze Age, but probably continued in use into the Iron Age and later. It is roughly oval in shape, but instead of being perforated, there may be a groove around the middle to hold thongs in position for the attachment of the handle. It is possible that this type of hammer was used in the extraction of copper, and the chance find of one might lead to the discovery of metalworking sites.

Also connected with metalworking are stone *moulds* which were used in casting copper and bronze artifacts. These may be flat pieces of stone in which were carved one or more shallow hollows in the shape of flat axe-heads and other simple metal artifacts. More elaborate forms reproduce, as it were in negative, every detail of more advanced bronze artifacts, such as socketed spearheads. Carefully worked blocks of stone may be found, square in cross-section, on each face of which there is a separate mould. Strictly speaking, of course, these more elaborate forms are really only halves of *two-piece moulds* which were necessary for casting anything but a simple, flat object.

Jet or lignite was used during the earlier part of the Bronze Age for personal ornaments. These include *conical buttons* with a V-shaped perforation in the flat base. Rings were made of the same substance, and these also had a number of V-shaped perforations around the circumference. They were probably used as belt-fasteners. The most elaborate jet object is a *necklace* made from numbers of oval beads and flat *spacer beads* which have a number of inter-connected perforations, and whose surfaces are sometimes decorated with a geometric pattern of punched dots.

Rotary querns may be found. When complete, they

comprise two large circular components, eighteen inches or more in diameter, which fit closely together. Each has a central perforation for an axle, and the upper may have one or more holes near the circumference for a wooden handle.   Their profiles vary from a bun-shaped cross-section to more flattened types, and this variation may be used to give a rough indication of date.   The former type may date from the Iron Age, but rotary querns continued in use during the Roman period and well into the Middle Ages.   Small, flat discs of stone, about two inches or so in diameter, and with a central perforation are *spindle whorls*, a kind of fly-wheel used to facilitate rotation of the spindle during spinning.   They are difficult to date unless found in an archaeological context, but the earliest may date from the Neolithic.

Roman inscriptions, altars and sculpture may, surprisingly, occur as casual finds, and their discovery in the past has led to the location of Romano-British buildings such as temples.   Interpretation of stone carvings of this type is a specialised study, but carvings are usually easy to recognise, even if fragmentary.   We examined some examples of stone carvings which may be found *in situ* (see above, page 79), but such standing stones may be broken and parts of them dispersed.

POTTERY

The study of early pottery, like that of flint, is of fundamental importance to the archaeologist.   Pottery was introduced into Britain and Ireland by immigrant farmers at the beginning of the Neolithic.   From that period pottery continued to be made on a domestic scale in southern Britain until the arrival of imported wares just before the Roman invasion.   Elsewhere, older traditions of potting continued into the post-Roman period. There was a temporary reversion to this tradition in southern Britain after the end of the Roman period.

Prehistoric pottery is important for two main reasons. In the first place, although a complete pot may be shattered, broken pieces of pottery, or *sherds*, generally survive well in a variety of soil conditions. They are rarely affected by extremely acidic or alkaline soils. Second, the making of prehistoric pottery was a domestic task, presumably undertaken by the woman of the house. Primitive communities, and here we may include prehistoric communities, generally tend to be conservative in their habits, and therefore the study of pottery and its variations and developments may lead to an understanding of cultural changes and connections. Although pottery was probably produced independently by different families or groups of families and not by full-time potters, within the community as a whole there would tend to be a certain uniformity of type and decoration at any given time. These points are stressed because the high survival value of pottery has allowed its study to form the basis of much of our knowledge of cultural changes and relationships during the prehistoric period.

Most finds of prehistoric and Romano-British pottery will be in the form of sherds. With experience it is possible to attribute even quite small sherds to their correct culture and period. It is not possible to describe in this book the many types of sherd which may be found in the British Isles. The field archaeologist should, as in the case of flint artifacts, learn from study in a museum the texture and colour of the main types of pottery which may be encountered in his area. There will be considerable variation in texture, both of the surface and the cross-section of different sherds. Some surfaces will be smooth and polished, others quite rough. Some will have little or no decoration, whereas other sherds may have much decoration made by impressions of such things as lengths of twisted cord, pieces of wood or bone, finger-nails and finger-tips. There may also be sherds with incised decoration arranged in triangles, lozenges or zigzags, and some may have grooves and applied bands of clay. The texture of the interior of the pot, as shown in cross-section, may vary from very fine, in which the whole texture is uniform, to coarse, in which there may be large lumps of quartz, flint or shell. Surface colours may vary from black to light grey and fawn, and from red to light brown. The colour of the surface may change even within the limits of a small sherd.

It is often possible to reconstruct from sherds the appearance of the original pot. To do this successfully certain parts of the pot may be necessary, and enough of the sherd or sherds should survive to give an indication of the diameter and curvature, if any, of the walls. Important features are rims, which may vary from simple to ledge-like forms, and bases, which may be flat or rounded. The walls of a pot may be curved or straight.

Complete pots may also appear as casual finds. While this book was being written, the author was called to a sand quarry where a very fine, intact Bronze Age pot had been found. The pot had appeared on a conveyor belt and apparently had been removed in a large quantity of sand by a mechanical excavator. It had then been dumped into a lorry load of sand and driven to the washing plant, where it appeared, having undergone the washing process! This not only illus-trates the strength of some prehistoric pottery but also

serves as a reminder that complete pots may be found
in unexpected circumstances.   This particular incident
also emphasised the importance of reporting finds.   In
this case the owner of the quarry reported the find and
so made it possible for the discovery of the pot to be
published in a local archaeological journal.   As it
happened, few pots of this type had previously been
recorded in that particular area, and so the find had the
additional value of adding another spot to the distribution map.   A field archaeologist may often further
archaeological interests in a quiet way by letting it be
known locally that he is interested in 'old things'.   He
may subsequently be inundated with all kinds of worth-
less rubbish, but not infrequently something of archaeological importance may appear.

Some of the major types of prehistoric pottery may
be noted.   During the Neolithic there were three main
categories.   The first two have round bases.   One
type generally has a fine, smooth surface and little or
no decoration which, when it does occur, is generally
in the form of fine incisions on the rim or shoulder.
Shapes are usually simple, bag-shaped pots, but some
have shoulders.   In the south of England this pottery
is known as *Windmill Hill ware,* but similar pottery has
been found throughout Britain and Ireland, where it is
sometimes referred to as *Western Neolithic, Neolithic A*
or *Primary Neolithic ware.*   The second type is *Peterborough ware,* and this is distinguished by decoration in
the form of impressions of cord, bone, finger-tips and
finger-nails over much of its surface.   The fabric is
generally coarse, and the principal type is a bowl with
a heavy rim and hollow neck.   The third major type
is known at present as *Rinyo-Clacton* pottery.   This has
a flat base, straight, outward-splaying sides and simple
rims.   Decoration may consist of broad, shallow

Fig. 43. Neolithic Pottery. *Upper:* Western Neolithic.
Centre: Peterborough. *Lower:* Rinyo-Clacton.

grooves, which may cover the entire external face of
the pot. Applied bands of clay may also form part of
the decoration. Peterborough and Rinyo-Clacton
wares are normally restricted to Britain. The names
given to these three types of pottery are taken from
sites where they were first recognised. Such sites are
referred to as *type sites*. A type site also frequently lends
its name to an archaeological culture (Fig. 43).

Beaker pottery appears during the transition from

the Neolithic to the Early Bronze Age. Two main
types may be distinguished, Bell Beakers and Necked
Beakers. The *Bell Beaker* has a smooth, S-shaped
profile and is normally ornamented over most of its

Fig. 44. *Upper:* Beakers. *Lower:* Food Vessels.

surface with horizontal bands of decoration, including
series of fine impressions made by a comb-like object
or fine cord. The type has a wide distribution. The
Necked Beaker has a straight, slightly flaring neck and a
globular body. Decoration often employs vertical
motives, including well marked zigzags. Cord ornament is not normally found. Beakers with relatively
short necks are found mostly in northern Britain, and
long-necked Beakers in southern Britain. Beakers are
normally well made, having relatively thin walls and a

smooth surface. They were apparently used as drinking vessels and are most commonly found in small
round barrows or small stone cists (Fig. 44).

Beakers were brought into Britain and Ireland by
newcomers who were probably concerned with the
introduction of metal. They soon became absorbed
by the native population, and the Beaker as a type was
therefore relatively short-lived. At this period descen-
dants of the native Neolithic people produced *Food
Vessels*, which were a development of some of the later
Neolithic wares. Two main types may be distinguished,
the *vase type* (sometimes called the *Yorkshire type*) and the
bowl (or *Irish*) type. The vase type has an inverted
conical shape and a heavy, flattened rim. The bowl
type is rounded. Both types are frequently profusely
decorated and often have one or more grooves which
encircle the body horizontally. Both types are widespread in Britain and Ireland (Fig. 44).

These gradually gave way to *cinerary urns*, as both
Beakers and Food Vessels disappeared. They have a
wide range in size, and a number of types may be
identified. The *collared urn* has a marked rim or collar
and is sometimes called an *overhanging-rim urn*. *Encrusted urns* and *cordoned urns* both have applied bands of
decoration, the latter arranged horizontally and the
former forming a variety of motives on the surface (Fig.
45). Cinerary urns were containers for cremated
bones. As a type they are widely distributed, but
encrusted and cordoned urns tend to be found more in
the highland areas of Britain and in Ireland. Towards
the end of the Bronze Age in southern Britain there were
three main types of urn. Two are of native derivation,
the *bucket urn* and the *barrel urn*, and one imported from
northern France, the less-common *globular urn*. The
two native types have little or no decoration, apart

from an applied horizontal band, which may have finger-tip ornament.

In the early part of the Iron Age in southern Britain two main types may be distinguished.   One is a small bowl, sometimes red in colour, with horizontal grooving, and the other is a taller, high-shouldered pot.   Later in the period regional variants appear which may be decorated with either incised curvilinear ornament or a variety of small impressions below the rim.   In northern

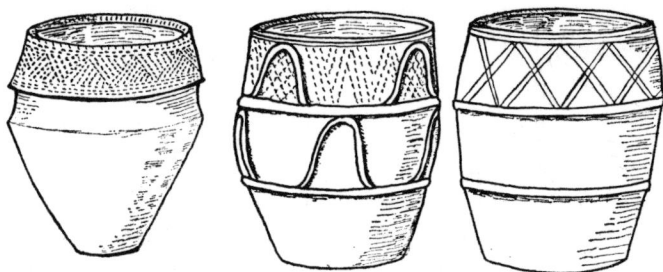

Fig. 45. Collared, encrusted and cordoned urn.

Britain and in Ireland less is known of the pottery of the Late Bronze Age and the Iron Age.   One of the distinctive pots of the final stages of the Iron Age in southern England is the tall, *pedestalled urn*, and this, in contrast with all the preceding types, was made on the fast potter's wheel.

During the Roman period a considerable variety of pottery was in use in southern Britain.   This included both imported and locally produced wares.   Among the former was *Samian ware*, common in the first two centuries A.D.   It may be distinguished by its fine red, glossy surface and its almost three-dimensional decoration of figures from classical mythology and other motives.   Pottery made in Britain includes a great deal of so-called *coarse wares*, purely utilitarian wheel-made pottery, but also finer wares. These include *Castor ware*, named after a site in Northamptonshire where it was produced. A common type was a drinking vessel, usually dark in colour, with a lighter-coloured applied decoration sometimes depicting incidents from hunting or gladiatorial contests. Castor ware has a wide distribution in the civil zone of south-east Britain. Another type is *New Forest ware*, which occurs in a variety of shapes and has painted decoration, usually in geometric or curvilinear patterns, and impressed rosettes.

METAL

(a) *Copper and Bronze*. Copper and bronze objects dating from the Bronze Age are easily identified, although without chemical analysis it is not always possible to determine whether certain Early Bronze Age objects were made of copper or bronze. Three main categories may be distinguished, and a typological development from simple to more advanced forms is apparent in each.

One of the earliest types of *dagger* is flat and rather broad. The hilt, which was normally of wood or bone, rarely survives, but was attached by rivets which commonly remain in position on the blade. The blade was gradually lengthened and provided with a central mid-rib for strength. This eventually developed into the *rapier*, a long, thrusting weapon, which had an inherent weakness in that the hilt was riveted to the blade. Towards the end of the Bronze Age continental types influenced local development with the introduction of a true *slashing sword*, which had a heavier blade suitable for slashing as well as thrusting. The hilt was cast in one piece with the blade, and the resultant sword was a weapon of some strength (Fig. 46).

The earliest type of copper or bronze *axe-head* was flat, but this was quickly followed by the *flanged axe*, in which the sides were hammered up into flanges to hold

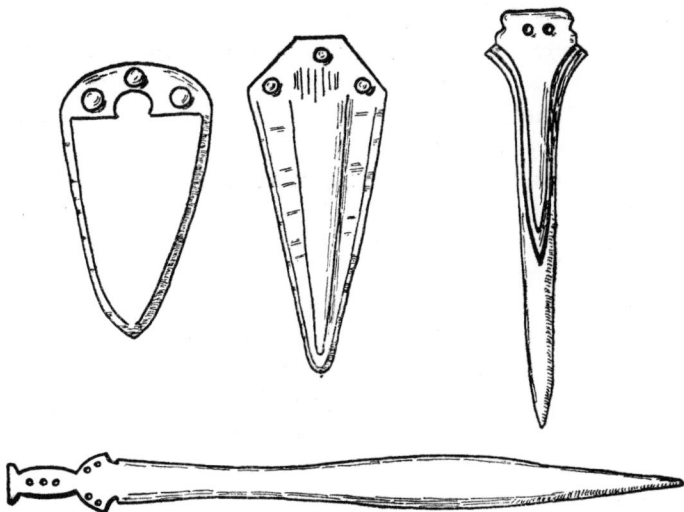

Fig. 46. *Upper:* daggers and rapier. *Lower:* sword.

the haft more securely in position. Flanges were later cast in one piece with the blade to produce the *cast-flanged axe*. Some of these axe-heads, particularly those made in Ireland, were decorated by incisions and punched ornament. To prevent the butt from splitting the haft a *stop-ridge* was cast about half-way along the axe-head. From this there developed the *palstave*, which had pronounced flanges and greater weight in the blade. *Looped palstaves* have one or two small loops for the attachment of thongs tying the palstave to its haft. Under continental influence during the

M

latter part of the Bronze Age the *winged axe* was introduced, in which the side flanges were extended to curve inwards and so grasped part of the haft. Parallel with this development was that of the *socketed axe*, in which the tip of the haft fitted firmly into a square or circular socket (Fig. 47).

The *spear head* appears to have developed initially from a *tanged dagger* which was mounted on a wooden shaft. A metal collar was sometimes used in place of cord to bind the end of the shaft. This collar was subsequently cast with the spear head, and it was then realised that the central tang was superfluous. It was omitted, and this produced the *socketed spear head*, some of which have small loops. Others were riveted on to the shaft (Fig. 48).

Towards the end of the Bronze Age metal became more plentiful and many more bronze types were produced, including wood-working tools, sickles and even razors. At the same time sheet bronze working was introduced and used to produce circular bronze *shields*, tall shouldered *buckets* and fine *cauldrons*. The buckets and cauldrons both had *ring handles* and cast bronze *staples* for their attachment. These are sometimes found broken from their vessels with small pieces of sheet bronze adhering to them.

The great bulk of bronze objects dating from the Bronze Age have been casual finds, and very few have been found during excavation. It is therefore important that the field archaeologist should be able to recognise the principal types. Sometimes an object may be brown or bronze-coloured, but its surface colour will often have been changed due to chemical action in the soil, and may have a green *patina*. Bronze objects may be found singly, but in the Late Bronze Age in particular may also be found in *hoards*, often

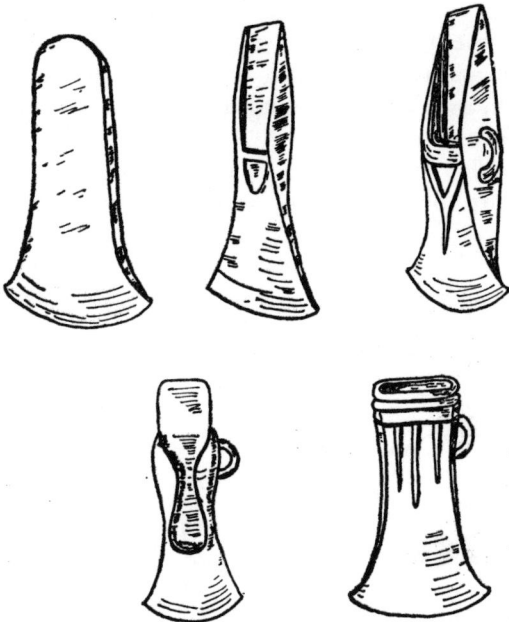

Fig. 47. Copper and bronze axeheads and palstaves.

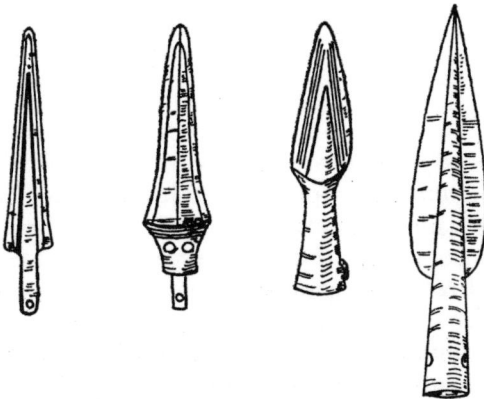

Fig. 48. Bronze spearheads.

including broken tools and weapons, pieces of moulds and fragments of ingots. These represent the stock in trade of a travelling smith or trader who had hidden his stock, usually by burying it, but who did not return to retrieve it.

With the introduction of iron, bronze came to be used more for decoration, and many fine examples of

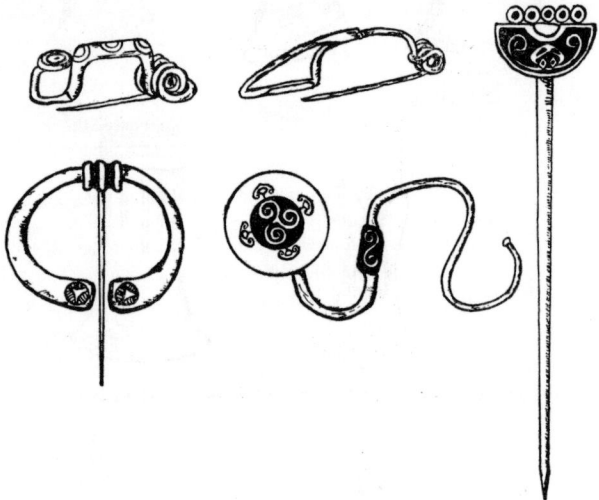

Fig. 49.

Celtic metal work have been found by chance. These include ornaments for horse harness and chariots, horse bits, fine helmets and shields, and mirrors with incised decoration. They are too numerous to describe here, and reference should be made to the books listed on page 202. A common find is the bronze safety-pin brooch or *fibula*, which may date from either the Iron Age or Roman period. There are many varieties, but the basic design remained constant, as may be seen on Fig. 49 *upper*. Another type is the *penannular brooch*, in which a movable pin is attached to a flat, circular strip of metal, the ends of which did not quite meet (Fig. 49, *bottom left*). Many fine examples of this type have been found in Ireland and western Britain, and its use continued well into the post-Roman period. *Latchet brooches* and *hand pins* of the Early Christian period may be found in Ireland (see Fig. 49, *lower* and *extreme right*).

(b) *Gold*. Gold ornaments were in use from the beginning of the Bronze Age. Many different types of neck ornament, bracelets and dress ornament are known, and as almost all have been casual finds, the field archaeologist should learn to recognise the more common types.

Neck ornaments include lunulae, gorgets and torcs. The *lunula* is the simplest and earliest type, and dates from the Early Bronze Age. It is a crescentic or moon-shaped (hence the name 'lunula') collar of thin sheet gold, and often has fine incised ornament. The majority of lunulae have been found in Ireland, but several are known from Britain. The gorget is also made of sheet gold, but ribs and sometimes cord-like ornament are beaten into it as decoration. A large saucer-shaped disc, often decorated with a series of finely incised concentric circles, was attached to each end.

The simplest form of *torc* is a thin twisted strip of gold. More elaborate types were also produced, but retained the effect of twisted gold. Both simple and elaborate types were made during the Middle and Late Bronze Ages, and normally had simple terminals. Even more elaborate torcs were worn in the Celtic Iron Age. The true torc is that which employs twisted metal, and some are made of multiple strands of gold wire. Others were tubular in section and were frequently decorated with

M2

embossed ornament. All Celtic torcs have prominent terminals, which may be disc or buffer-like (*buffer torcs*) or rings. Torcs of similar size and decoration were also made from bronze. Gold and bronze bracelets were often made to the same design as torcs.

Small sheet *gold plaques*, rectangular or lozenge-shaped, have been found in some Early Bronze Age barrows, and appear to have been sewn on to clothing. They are relatively rare. *Dress fasteners*, dating to the later part of the Bronze Age, are more common. They are approximately semicircular bars of gold with prominent expanding terminals.

In addition to these main types of gold ornament, *ear-rings* and *hair-fasteners* may be found. Mention must also be made of *coins*, both Celtic and Roman, which were made of bronze and gold, and silver also in the case of Roman. Like bronze objects, gold artifacts may be found both singly and in hoards.

(c) *Iron.* Casual finds of iron objects will be less common than those of bronze, as iron which has been exposed to the atmosphere will corrode relatively quickly and either disappear completely or become corroded into an unrecognisable mass. Iron objects may, however, be found during peat cutting or drainage, but may be difficult to date. The metal was used primarily for everyday tools and weapons. During the Iron Age the basic design of tools, such as chisels, gouges and saws, was developed to a stage close to that of today. Casual finds of recognisable iron objects should be submitted to a museum for expert identification. Many may be of recent date, but a museum curator would gladly examine any such object, even though it might be modern, rather than lose the opportunity of acquiring a more ancient artifact. Even apparently unrecognisable lumps of corroded iron should similarly be reported, as it is sometimes possible to remove corrosion, and so reveal the underlying object.

PERISHABLE SUBSTANCES

From the Palaeolithic period onwards objects were made from wood, bone and antler and possibly leather. Baskets woven from grasses and reeds were also prob-

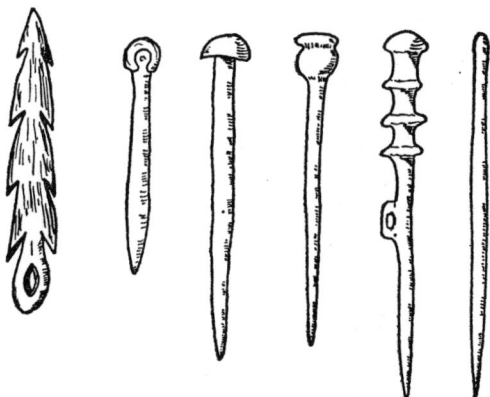

Fig. 50. Harpoon head (*extreme left*) and bone pins.

ably in common use from a later period. Relatively little of this material has survived, but the frequency with which these materials were used will immediately be appreciated when one realises that arrowheads, axeheads and daggers, for example, all had wooden shafts, hafts and hilts.

Bone and antler objects which survive include various types of missile points, including barbed *harpoon heads*. The latter were used by hunting and fishing communities during the latter part of the Palaeolithic and during the Mesolithic periods, and may be found in or near lakes, rivers and on the sea coast. *Pins* for fastening clothing and for holding hair in position may occasionally survive. Some are quite simple, skewer-like objects, and others have elaborately carved heads. Needles and awls, scrapers and combs of various types survive from different periods (Fig. 50).

Objects of *wood* may vary in size from an axe haft to a *dug-out canoe* fashioned from a tree-trunk. Few of the former have been found in Britain, but many dug-out canoes have been discovered in rivers and lakes. Wooden *shields*, similar in size to circular shields of bronze referred to above have been found in Ireland, and similar shields are also known to have been made of leather, and at least one has been found in Ireland. Rather more *leather* objects of Roman date have been found in Britain, and these include shoes and even what has been referred to as a 'bikini'.

HOW TO DEAL WITH CASUAL FINDS

The archaeological value of a casual find is lost if details of it are not circulated as widely and as soon as possible after discovery. In the case of more important finds, such as those of complete or nearly complete pots, metal objects, including coins, and more important stone artifacts, this will probably mean publication in an archaeological journal. The finder himself may be able to do this, but if not, the curator of his local museum or the secretary of the local archaeological society will put him in touch with someone who can. If an object, such as a single flint artifact or sherd of common type, is not sufficiently important to merit separate publication its discovery should be reported to the nearest museum. In this way a record is kept of all finds, and in time sufficient data might be collected for a detailed study of the type to be made and for possible publication. Accurate distribution maps can be compiled only if adequate records of all finds are made.

The position of any find must be accurately recorded. It is not sufficient to note that a find came from 'such and such a field' or 'on the banks of river X'. A full grid reference should be given, if possible as an eight-figure grid reference (see above, page 26). This is necessary, as it is possible that similar finds might subsequently be made near by, and the spatial inter-relationship of such finds might provide clues leading to the location of a buried site. If a find is made on the ground surface, say, after ploughing or on moorland, a note should be made of the type of soil and vegetation in the area. A note should also be made of the surroundings of a find made during digging and building work, peat cutting or in a river bank, and the depth of the find below ground level should be carefully measured. It may often be of value to take a small sample of soil or peat surrounding a buried find.

If a find should be made on a recognisable archaeological site the temptation to dig holes or remove any stone structure in the hope of making further discoveries must strongly be resisted. It is quite possible that collapse of stone on some fortified sites or cairns might uncover artifacts. If so, the relationship of the find to the structure should most carefully be noted and wherever possible be accompanied by a detailed plan or a sketch. A photograph of the object before it has been removed would also be of considerable value. If the finder suspects that more artifacts lie near by and close to the surface this should *immediately* be reported to the secretary of the local archaeological society or to the nearest museum, as it might be possible to organise an immediate rescue excavation.

Most artifacts which may appear as casual finds will normally, on discovery, be lying loosely on the ground surface. They may be found lying in a newly ploughed field, in shifting sand or at the bottom of a trench. They may possibly be covered by loose soil or stone, but they are not normally firmly embedded in the ground. This means that they may safely be lifted without damage. If, however, an artifact should be found partially buried, care should be taken in its removal. On no account must the object be pulled out of the ground, as it might break. Any earth or stone which traps the object must be carefully removed. In a proper archaeological excavation a small pointing trowel would be used, but a pen-knife or something similar would be adequate to scrape away any surrounding earth. A similar technique should be used in removing an artifact exposed in the face of a quarry or in a river bank. It must be emphasised that embedded artifacts should be removed by a person who has no experience of archaeological excavation technique only in an emergency. Clearly, if an object is in a prominent position so that it is likely to be noticed by passers-by, or if it lies in the path of a bulldozer or is in ground about to be disturbed in any way, then its immediate removal is necessary. If at all possible the object should be protected in some way, perhaps by covering it with fine, loose earth until it can be examined *in situ* by an experienced archaeologist. There is always the possibility that such an object may be lying in an important archaeological context. If so, its removal, whenever possible, should be part of a proper archaeological excavation. If this is impossible, then very particular note should be taken of the surrounding area; the type of soil, any traces of stone structure or timber, colour changes in the soil, both horizontal and vertical, and any evidence of burning, particularly charcoal, which should also be collected. Measured drawings, sketches and photographs should supplement written descriptions whenever possible.

The condition of artifacts when first discovered may vary considerably. Objects of flint and other stone will normally be quite firm, but if an artifact should be found to be broken the surrounding area should be examined for the remainder. The breakage might have been recent, particularly if the object is found on a building site or the like. Sherds of pottery will frequently be firm enough to be handled on discovery, although great care must be taken in subsequent transport and storage. Tobacco tins make useful containers for small sherds, which should be wrapped in tissue (paper handkerchiefs are satisfactory) and packed in cotton-wool. Sherds found in damp conditions may themselves be damp and perhaps pliable. They should be handled very carefully and allowed to dry slowly as soon as they have been taken to a safe place. A complete pot will require the careful handling necessary for any type of pottery. Should a pot be discovered to be broken but complete, an attempt should be made to remove it in such a way that the broken pieces remain in correct relationship to each other. Such a pot will normally have a filling of some sort, which should not be removed, as it might contain bone or even other artifacts, and will support the pot during removal and transport. A broad bandage should be wound gently but firmly around the outside of the pot. If bandage is not available strips of newspaper may be used. In either case several thicknesses should be applied over as large an area as possible. In lifting the pot care should be taken to support the underside. A sheet of thin metal would be useful, such as the detachable base of a baking tin, but if two or more persons are available, a flat shovel or spade may be used. A piece of plywood or even stiff cardboard would serve if there was nothing else available. The pot should then be placed in a strong cardboard box and packed carefully with well-crumpled newspaper.

Copper, bronze and gold objects will normally be quite firm, and can be removed with little difficulty. If incomplete when found, the surrounding area should be examined for any missing pieces. Copper and bronze may be corroded and if so, must be handled carefully. Any detached pieces of corroded metal should also be collected. Iron objects are more commonly corroded, and are often very fragile. They should be handled with great care, and once lifted from the ground should be very carefully wrapped in tissue and packed in a strong container for transport. Artifacts made from perishable substances, such as wood and leather, are likely to be fragile, and there is always the danger that they might be destroyed in removal. As they most commonly survive in damp conditions, they should be kept in similarly moist conditions until they can be treated properly by an expert. A useful method is to pack any such object in quantities of damp newspaper or moss, and this packing itself should be kept moist until delivered to a museum.

On no account should an attempt be made to clean any object. Loose earth may be lightly brushed from the surface with a soft brush, but wire brushes or files, for example, should never be used on a metal object— as has happened so often. Any deposit of soil in, say, a socket should be left undisturbed until it can be examined scientifically.   Pottery, and particularly prehistoric pottery, should not be vigorously brushed with a hard brush.

Although many casual finds of artifacts are made annually, the problem of dealing with partially buried objects and very fragile ones will arise much less frequently.   If such circumstances arise, the finder should as soon as possible ask for help from the nearest competent museum.

In conclusion, we must refer to the legal position concerning casual finds.   In England and Wales anything found legally belongs to the landowner, except in the case of Treasure Trove.   He should therefore be notified, otherwise the finder could be prosecuted for larceny.   A landowner might be willing to allow the finder to keep the more commonly found artifacts, such as flint arrowheads, but would probably wish to retain a bronze object.

Objects of gold and silver are covered by the law of *Treasure Trove*.   This is rather complicated, but briefly it means that objects of gold and silver which had been hidden and not subsequently recovered by their owner become the property of the Crown.   Objects which were lost or abandoned by their original owner belong to the owner of the land on which they were found. The decision as to whether such objects had been hidden or abandoned is made by a coroner's jury, and all finds of gold and silver must be reported immediately to the police.   If the Crown takes possession of the finds for exhibition in the British Museum in London or the National Museum of Wales in Cardiff or another museum the finder and not the landowner (unless he is the same person) receives their full market value, and not merely the value of the metal itself.   Apart from gold and silver, finds made on common land may normally be retained by the finder. The law in Northern Ireland is similar, but finds of treasure trove remain in the Province and will probably be exhibited in the Ulster Museum, Belfast.

In Scotland the position is less complicated, as all finds, whether of gold or silver or not, are treasure trove and on discovery automatically belong to the Crown. The National Museum of Antiquities (Queen Street, Edinburgh, 2) should be notified of all finds, and will normally retain most of the more important, although less important finds, other than those of gold and silver, may be returned to the landowner.

In the Republic of Ireland all archaeological finds, both artifacts and newly identified structures, such as cists and souterrains, must be reported either to the Gardaí or the Keeper of Irish Antiquities in the National Museum of Ireland (Kildare Street, Dublin, 2). The more important objects will normally be retained by the Museum, but the finder or landowner may be paid a small sum of money.

It is possible, then, despite the operation of these different laws and the rights of landowners, that the field archaeologist may legally find himself in possession of some ancient objects. What should he do with them? The most sensible thing would be to present them to a museum, and preferably to the museum nearest to the place where the objects were found. This means that the objects would be properly stored, catalogued, possibly exhibited and always available for examination. The day of large private collections is rapidly passing, but if a young field archaeologist wished to build up a small collection of, say, flint implements there would be few objections, provided he followed certain rules.

He should first report all finds to the nearest museum so that details of them may be recorded. This will also ensure that if an object is of exceptional importance the museum curator will persuade the finder or landowner to present it to the museum! The collector should then carefully catalogue his finds, as the time might come when he may wish to present his whole collection to a museum. He should number all his finds, perhaps using his initials followed by a serial number, e.g. JC:10. His catalogue would include a full description of the object, including dimensions and preferably a drawing, alongside the relevant catalogue number. There should also be an account of the circumstances of discovery, including the date when found. It is important that the catalogue number should also appear on the artifact itself. If the surface is smooth and suitable this may easily be printed in very small characters in black or white drawing ink (according to whether the artifact is light or dark in colour) directly on to a convenient part of the surface, preferably in a position which is as unobtrusive as possible. If the surface is too rough to take ink directly a small rectangular area should be painted with either water-colour varnish or *plain* nail varnish. When dry, it will take drawing ink quite easily. When the lettering has dried it should be carefully painted over with a thin coat of varnish to prevent its being rubbed off. Museums use various chemicals for this purpose, but these may be difficult to buy locally in small quantities, whereas a small bottle of one of these varnishes may be obtained quite easily. A small bottle will be sufficient for use on several hundred artifacts, and may be obtained quite cheaply. Should a private collection eventually be presented to a museum, the lettering and varnish may easily be removed to make room for the museum's own catalogue number to be applied.

Cataloguing artifacts may seem remote from field archaeology, but a keen field archaeologist in many parts of Britain and Ireland may find himself acquiring a small collection. If a young field archaeologist enjoys making his catalogue he may decide to make a career of museum work. If he has no intention of making a careful catalogue he should not keep any artifacts in his possession!

CHAPTER X

Taking it Further

WE have now examined the principal types of field monument which survive in Britain and Ireland, and the most common prehistoric artifacts which may be found by chance in these islands. Recognition and study of such monuments and artifacts are an important part of field archaeology, but their interpretation and study are more properly indoor activities. One very important archaeological activity, excavation, cannot adequately be dealt with in a book. One can really learn the essentials of excavation technique only by taking part in a number of excavations. One has, in fact, to serve an archaeological apprenticeship. The overall interpretation of archaeological data may be achieved only after acquiring a thorough grounding in the Archaeology of these islands, together with some knowledge of the European background. In this final chapter we shall briefly examine some of the means by which a young field archaeologist may begin to do these things.

The study of, and participation in, Archaeology may be pursued on many different levels. Some readers of this book may be content to simply visit sites and museums in order to learn and appreciate what is already known. Others may wish to take some active part in extending archaeological knowledge. One means of doing this is by joining a local archaeological society. There are many such societies in Britain and

Ireland, and several have either special sections for younger members or offer a reduced membership fee. A young archaeologist should never feel that it would be presumptuous of him to think of applying for membership. Most societies are most anxious to welcome young members to ensure that their society's activities will continue in the future. All archaeologists, no matter how venerable and distinguished they may be today, were once beginners, and if one has leanings towards any subject it is surely desirable that this interest should be fostered from as early a date as possible.

Membership of a society offers many benefits. Most societies organise a number of evening lectures during the winter months, usually held once a month. These may include accounts of excavations, often local excavation, and discussions of problems of wider interest within the county or region generally. There may also be lectures dealing with wider aspects of Archaeology which concern Britain and Ireland as a whole. The membership fee will also often entitle the member to receive the society's annual publication (which may be called *Journal*, *Transactions*, *Collections* or *Proceedings*). In this he will be able to study recent work on the Archaeology of his area. Many societies organise, during the summer, visits to sites of archaeological interest, and it is normal for a talk to be given at the different sites visited. Societies may also arrange excavations, including training excavations, in which members are invited to take part. Some societies, too, have their own libraries of archaeological books and journals which are available on loan to members. Finally, membership of an archaeological society brings one into contact with other people of similar interests, and this will encourage the exchange of information and knowledge.

Many societies are organised on a county basis, and some have been in existence for more than a century. Others have been formed more recently and may be primarily concerned with the Archaeology of an area more limited than a county. The name and address of the secretary of the nearest society may normally be obtained from the local Public Library, which will often advertise a society's lecture and excursion programme. Failing this, the relevant information may be obtained from the Secretary, Council for British Archaeology, 4 St. Andrew's Place, Regent's Park, London, N.W.1.

The young archaeologist may feel that he would like to take part during his summer holidays in an excavation in a part of the country away from his home. This will apply particularly to those whose local societies may not be organising an excavation and to those who live in an area not served by a society. If so, he will find useful the *Calendar of Excavations* which is issued monthly from March to September by the C.B.A. (the usual abbreviation for the Council for British Archaeology). It may be available for study in the local Public Library, or a year's issue may be obtained for five shillings from the C.B.A. at the above address. The *Calendar* lists all excavations at which volunteers would be welcomed. At most excavations it will be necessary for volunteers to pay for their own accommodation, but it is often possible to camp on or near the site, and reasonably priced accommodation may be found locally. Some excavators, however, offer a financial contribution towards accommodation. The *Calendar* also lists excavations which are specifically planned to train beginners in excavation technique. It should be emphasised that many excavators will gladly welcome young people, and it must also be remembered that on an excavation no one will be asked to do anything beyond his capabilities. A young archaeologist will not be expected to undertake skilled tasks until he is experienced, and then only under close supervision. He will not be asked to handle heavy tools if he is not capable of doing so—after all, a trowel and a hand-brush are used on an archaeological excavation at least as often as a pick and shovel!

In addition to details of excavation the *Calendar* also gives details of residential courses on Archaeology which do not include excavation. These may take the form of a week or fortnight's summer school or a shorter week-end course, and will generally include visits to museums and archaeological sites. Some are specially designed for young people, such as those organised by Field Study Centres and the Youth Hostels Association (Y.H.A.). In one of these ways the young archaeologist will gradually be led on to the systematic study of Archaeology, which he may supplement by attending lectures organised by his local society and by his own reading.

We have not discussed any archaeological activities which may form part of school work, as we are concerned here only with out-of-school activities. Some schools do organise excavations, and many visit museums and archaeological sites. In some areas, notably in Wales, a Schools Museum Service lends small collections of antiquities for exhibition in schools. Many schools also have their own archaeological societies.

After leaving school the young field archaeologist may wish to continue with his interest in Archaeology. He may do so by studying the subject at a University. This may be taken either as a principal subject or as part of a degree course, and if he would like to do this his headmaster is the best person to consult. If he should take a degree in Archaeology he may wish to make a career as an archaeologist, although he will probably be warned that there are very few full-time posts. It is also possible to make a career in the museum service without having a degree, although this will naturally involve other professional training.

Archaeology, however, is a subject which has room for both full-time or professional archaeologists and for amateurs or part-time archaeologists. The word 'amateur' today unfortunately sometimes tends to be used disparagingly, but strictly speaking, an amateur is one who loves his subject for its own sake. Some of the best archaeological work has been achieved and is being achieved by amateurs, and there should be no difference in the quality of work accomplished by amateurs or professionals. If an amateur is unable to reach an acceptable standard in a specific task he should not attempt it—any more than should a professional. Fortunately there is much that the amateur may do, both as an individual and as a member of his local society. Earlier in this book we saw that a young field archaeologist might begin by studying the Archaeology of his immediate area or might concentrate on some particular types of field monuments. In doing so he might discover new sites or be able to make a detailed study of some aspect of his local Archaeology. There are many parts of Britain and Ireland which have received little detailed study, and there is plenty of room for the amateur to contribute his local knowledge.

If the young archaeologist wishes to continue his interest in the subject without making a career of Archaeology he will naturally remain a member of his local society and perhaps begin to take an active part in its activities. He may wish to join one of the national societies which he will learn of through his local society. Evening classes in Archaeology, and not merely local studies, are arranged in many parts of Britain and Ireland, and details of these may be obtained from the Local Library. A short reading list is printed at the end of this book. Some of these books may be in the Local Library and possibly in the school library. Books which are not available locally either on loan or for reference may be borrowed from other libraries through the Local Library, and the librarian will be able to arrange for this. Wherever possible, visits should be made to museums. Frequent short visits are preferable to prolonged infrequent visits, as one may quickly suffer from archaeological indigestion. Only by seeing actual objects can one really learn their true appearance. A museum curator will normally be only too anxious to give all possible help to anyone he knows to be genuinely interested in Archaeology. The young archaeologist may therefore count on help being available to him whenever he needs it.

The author of this little book hopes that it may be of some use to those young people who may be attracted to Archaeology. An early interest in the subject may lead to a satisfying life-long hobby, although this is too flimsy a word to describe a subject which offers so much of interest. It is a subject which gives the opportunity to contribute something to the knowledge of our past, whether by excavation, detailed study of particular problems or by the planning and recording of field antiquities. The basis of all archaeological knowledge, however, must always rest on field work. This is an aspect of the subject which combines the delights of working in the open air in some of the most attractive parts of these islands, training in the powers of observation and the intellectual excitement of piecing together small clues to provide answers to specific problems relating to the past.

Reading List

MANY books have been published on ancient monuments, and some of those listed here will help field archaeologists to locate individual sites. The Ministry of Public Building and Works publish six excellent and inexpensive *Illustrated Guides to Ancient Monuments*. Three volumes cover England (I, *Northern England*, II, *Southern England* and III, *East Anglia and Midlands*), two are devoted to Wales (IV, *South Wales* and V, *North Wales*) and Volume VI covers *Scotland*. As they are designed to guide one to sites which are in the care of the Ministry, they include the more visually impressive sites of all periods. The Ministry also publishes illustrated booklets devoted to smaller areas than those covered by the *Guides* proper, such as those on *Anglesey*, *Orkney* and *Hadrian's Wall*. Guides to individual sites are also published.

Northern Ireland is covered in a similar way by two booklets published by Her Majesty's Stationery Office, *Ancient Monuments of Northern Ireland in State Charge* and *Ancient Monuments in Northern Ireland not in State Charge*. For the Republic of Ireland there is *The National Monuments of Ireland*, published by Bord Failte Eireann. This also includes details of twenty-five monuments in Northern Ireland.

Publication dates of these guides are not given as they are constantly revised and new editions appear frequently. They all include the location and description of each site, maps, plans and illustrations, and a general archaeological background.

Several guides which include details of many sites not included in official guides have also been published. Two have been published by Batsford: *A Guide to Prehistoric England*, by Nicholas Thomas (1960), and *A Guide to Prehistoric Scotland*, by Richard Feachem (1963). There is also Jacquetta Hawkes' *A Guide to the Prehistoric and Roman Monuments of England and Wales* (Chatto and Windus, 1951). Seán P. Ó Ríordáin's *Antiquities of the Irish Countryside* (Methuen, 1953, and now in paperback) is less of a guide and more a series of essays on the more important field monuments of Ireland. Many archaeological sites in Ireland are described in the *Shell Guide to Ireland*, by Lord Killanin and Michael V. Duignan (Ebury Press, 1962).

Three useful series of books which deal with the Archaeology of either a county or small area have been, or are being, published. The first is Methuen's *County Archaeologies*, all published before 1939 and therefore a little out of date, but still useful. They are: *Berkshire*, by Harold Peake (1931); *Cornwall and Scilly*, by H. O'N. Hencken (1932); *Kent*, by R. F. Jessup (1930); *Middlesex and London*, by C. E. Vulliamy (1930); *Somerset*, by D. P. Dobson (1931); *Surrey*, by D. H. Whimster (1931); *Sussex*, by G. C. Curwen (1938); and *Yorkshire*, by F. and H. W. Elgee (1933). A second, revised edition of the *Archaeology of Sussex* was published in 1954. Thames and Hudson, in their wide-ranging series, *Ancient Peoples and Places*, include volumes on Britain and Ireland. Those published are Aileen Fox on *South West England* (1964), J. F. S. Stone on *Wessex before the Celts* (1958), R. R. Clarke on *East Anglia* (1960) and S. P. Ó Ríordáin and Glyn Daniel on *New Grange* (1964). Forthcoming volumes will cover *Central England*
N

(Adrian Oswald and Nicholas Thomas) and *Wales* (W. F. Grimes). The third series is Cory, Adams and Mackay's *Regional Archaeologies*. Volumes so far published are: *The Severn Basin*, by K. S. Painter (1964); *Yorkshire*, by Ian Longworth; and *North Wales*, by Katherine Watson (both published in 1965). Future volumes will cover *South Wales, South-west Scotland, Wessex, London* and the *Roman Frontiers of Britain*.

Two outstanding books on regional Archaeology are L. V. Grinsell's *The Archaeology of Wessex* (Methuen, 1958) and Sir Cyril Fox's pioneer work in local archaeological studies, *The Archaeology of the Cambridge Region* (Cambridge University Press, 1948).

In each of the books referred to in the last two paragraphs mention is made of artifacts, but perhaps the most useful books for helping one to learn the shapes of the more important artifacts are British Museum *Guides*. Two have been published which refer specifically to Britain and Ireland: *Later Prehistoric Antiquities of the British Isles* (1953) and *Guide to the Antiquities of Roman Britain* (1951). Of particular interest for earlier periods is *Flint Implements, An Account of Stone Age Techniques and Cultures* (1950). The National Museum of Ireland publishes *A Brief Guide to the Collection of Irish Antiquities*, by Joseph Raftery (1960). A valuable little booklet is the well-illustrated *English Prehistoric Pottery* (Small Picture Book No. 26), published by the Victoria and Albert Museum, London (1952).

Because of the rapidly changing nature of archaeological knowledge there are few up-to-date books on British and Irish Archaeology. The standard work for the prehistoric period remains V. G. Childe's *Prehistoric Communities of the British Isles* (Chambers, 1949). Smaller works include Stuart Piggott's *British Prehistory* (Oxford University Press, 1949) and J. and C. Hawkes'

Prehistoric Britain (Penguin, 1958). More restricted geographically, but still useful, is Grahame Clark's *Prehistoric England* (Batsford, 1948, and now in paperback).

A good introduction to Roman Britain is I. A. Richmond's *Roman Britain* (Penguin, 1955). Bridging this period and that of Anglo-Saxon England is Peter Hunter Blair's *Roman Britain and Early England* (Nelson, 1963). Three of Thames and Hudson's *Ancient Peoples and Places* series also deal with the post-Roman period: *Celtic Britain*, by Nora K. Chadwick (1963); *The Anglo-Saxons*, by D. M. Wilson (1960); and *Early Christian Ireland*, by Máire and Liam de Paor (1958). A classic of British Archaeology which must be read by every field archaeologist is Sir Cyril Fox's *Personality of Britain* (National Museum of Wales, Cardiff, 1952). This sets the Archaeology of Britain against its physical background.

A number of books dealing with specialised aspects of field work may be mentioned. For chambered cairns see G. E. Daniel's *Prehistoric Chamber Tombs of England and Wales* (Cambridge University Press, 1950), A. S. Henshall's *The Chambered Tombs of Scotland*, Volume I (Edinburgh University Press, 1963—Volume II forthcoming) and the first of a series for Ireland, *Survey of the Megalithic Tombs of Ireland*, Volume I, *Co. Clare*, by Ruaidhrí de Valera and Seán Ó Nualláin (Stationery Office, Dublin, 1961). For unchambered barrows see L. V. Grinsell's *Ancient Burial Mounds of England* (Methuen, 1953) and Paul Ashbee's *The Bronze Age Round Barrow in Britain* (Phoenix House, 1960). Despite its title, the latter also discusses Irish material. Celtic metalwork is discussed in Sir Cyril Fox's *Pattern and Purpose: Early Celtic Art in Britain* (National Museum of Wales, Cardiff, 1958).

Important aspects of Roman Britain referred to in this book include the Roman Army, for which Graham Webster's pamphlet *The Roman Army* (Grosvenor Museum, Chester, 1956) is a good introduction. Roman roads are discussed in detail in I. D. Margary's two volumes on *Roman Roads in Britain* (Phoenix House, 1955 and 1957). A. L. F. Rivet's book on *Town and Country in Roman Britain* (Hutchinson, 1958) is an excellent introduction to problems of villas and Romano-British towns. There is a useful hand-book to *The Antonine Wall*, by Anne S. Robertson (Glasgow Archaeological Society, 1960).

A useful book on Architecture, inexpensive and convenient to carry, is *The Observer's Book of Architecture*, by John Penoyre and Michael Ryan (Warne, no date of publication). The *Illustrated Guides to Ancient Monuments*, published by the Ministry of Public Building and Works and referred to above, include information on castles, abbeys and other architectural remains. The Ministry also publish four guides uniform with the *Illustrated Guides*. They are *Scottish Castles, An introduction to the Castles of Scotland*; and *Castles, An Introduction to the Castles of England and Wales*; *Scottish Abbeys, An introduction to the mediaeval Abbeys and Priories of Scotland*; and *Abbeys, An introduction to the Religious Houses of England and Wales*. For more detailed study in England, Penguin Books publish a fine series by Nikolaus Pevsner, *The Buildings of England*, each volume dealing with a county or part of a county.

The standard work on *Industrial Archaeology* is the book of that name by Kenneth Hudson (John Baker, 1963).

In conclusion, readers of this book will find interesting Geoffrey Bibby's *The Testimony of the Spade* (Collins, 1957), in which he describes some of the more important discoveries of European Archaeology. Those who would like to read of excavation technique should read Sir Mortimer Wheeler's *Archaeology from the Earth* (Oxford University Press, 1954). Some aspects of field work in general are discussed by one of the pioneers of the technique in Britain, O. G. S. Crawford, in his *Archaeology in the Field* (Phoenix House, 1953).

Index

In those entries where references are given figures in bold type (e.g. **37**) the latter refer either to definitions or to the most important single reference.